David Peaty

D1147236

LONGMAN

Addison Wesley Longman Limited
Edinburgh Gate
Harlow
Essex
CM20 2JE, England
and Associated Companies throughout the world.

© David Peaty 1983
First published by Thomas Nelson and Sons Ltd 1983

ISBN 0-17-555418-8
This impression Addison Wesley Longman Ltd 1996

Phototypeset by Tradespools Ltd, Frome, Somerset

Produced through Longman Malaysia, BVS

CONTENTS

INTRODUCTION

Working with English Idioms presents and practises over 800 idioms in a highly systematic way.

TO THE TEACHER

Idiomatic English presents many difficulties for the learner. Rules governing usage and range of application can be obscure or non-existent. Some expressions are used only in formal situations. Others are colloquial or slang. Some have both literal and idiomatic functions. Others have various meanings, depending on context. These problems can frustrate learners who are otherwise quite competent in English.

Idioms may be categorised in various ways according to similarities of structure, image, context and so on. Structural organisation is the most efficient system because it presents idioms in clearly-defined groups about which generalisations regarding structural adaptability may be made. *Working with English Idioms* uses this system.

In order to avoid the necessity of distinguishing between formal, neutral, colloquial and slang expressions, only common idioms which may be used in normal situations are included. These idioms are neither inhibitingly formal nor embarrassingly colloquial.

Many idioms have various unrelated meanings and functions. We have treated each meaning or function as belonging to a separate idiom. Only the most common meanings of such idioms are presented.

As far as possible, definitions and examples which involve the use of other idioms or of obscure language have been avoided. Idioms which have no exact literal equivalent are better understood by reference to examples. Wherever possible, idioms with opposite or parallel meanings are presented in close sequence in order that they may be more easily understood.

Many idioms, both common and uncommon, have been excluded from this text for practical reasons. It is clear, therefore, that an ability to guess the meaning of an idiom from its context is of great value to the learner. In most units there is a section which presents idioms without definition to be understood from their context alone and later checked with definitions in the key.

A few very common idioms which are self-explanatory and which will have already been learned as ordinary vocabulary, for example *stand up, sit down,* have been omitted.

This book may be used either for reference or in class as the basis for a comprehensive course on idiomatic English.

TO THE STUDENT

An idiom is an expression which cannot be understood from the literal meaning of the words of which it is composed. For example, *give in* is an idiom meaning 'surrender'. This idiomatic meaning is completely unrelated to the literal meanings of the individual words *give* and *in*.

Sometimes it is difficult to distinguish idiomatic usage from literal usage. Compare the following sentences

He came by bicycle.

He came by a bicycle.

In the second sentence, the idiom *come by*, meaning 'acquire', is used.

Idioms should always be learned in context. Sometimes their form is unchangeable. For example, *fed up* has no active form. Sometimes they may refer only to certain limited groups of objects. For example, *up to* is used with people but not things. Sometimes they have different meanings, depending on factors such as the position of the object. For example, *see (something) through* has an entirely different meaning than *see through (something)*.

Idioms may be formal, neutral, colloquial or slang. For example, *pass away* is a formal idiom meaning 'die'. It is only used when speaking to relatives of the dead person. *Kick the bucket* is a slang expression also meaning 'die' and is only used humorously between friends. Most of the idioms presented in this text are neutral and may be used in ordinary situations.

Some idioms have various meanings, depending on the context. For example, *take off* may be used with clothes, weight, prices, mimicry and aeroplanes. In each case, it has an entirely different meaning.

The idioms are presented in groups of ten, and each group has exercises based on it. These exercises provide thorough practice and will help you to use idioms with confidence.

HOW TO USE THIS BOOK

THE UNITS

The book is organised in twenty units, each one covering a different type of idiom. The idioms are categorised according to their grammatical structure, apart from the expressions in Units 16 and 20.

Each unit is introduced by short notes on the type of idiom to be practised. Read these notes carefully before going on to the exercises.

Most of the units contain forty idioms divided into four sections. Each idiom is presented with its meaning (with possible examples of contexts where it might be used in brackets) and an example of usage. Where an idiom has a meaning other than the one being practised, it is marked ☆. The other meanings tend to be less common, but you may wish to look them up in a dictionary.

Each set of ten idioms has related exercises, which appear on the same page, providing thorough practice of the idioms and consolidating your understanding of them.

THE EXERCISES

There are seven standard exercise types which appear throughout the book. Instructions on how to do each exercise are given here. Read these instructions carefully before beginning work on the idioms.

Ask and answer

Here you are given a question to answer, using the appropriate idiom. A prompt is sometimes given in brackets and sometimes you have to choose from the ten idioms presented in the section.

Complete the sentence

Here you are given an unfinished sentence to complete, using the appropriate idiom. Occasionally, the gap to be completed appears in the middle of the sentence. Prompts are sometimes given.

Find the idiom

This type of exercise gives sentences which suggest, but do not contain, the idioms you have just studied. You have to find the appropriate idiom by comparing the examples in the presentation section with the exercise sentences.

Work it out

This usually appears as the final section of each unit. The idioms are presented without their meanings. Try to work out the meaning from the example sentence, and then write your own definition. Answers to the *Work it out* exercises are provided in a key at the back of this book.

In your own words

Here you are given sentences which suggest the idioms you have just studied. You have to choose the appropriate idiom (sometimes with the help of prompts) and then use it to rewrite the sentence.

On your own

This exercise appears at the end of each section and suggests extra practice to do at home.

Join the sentences

Here you are given two short sentences and a prompt. Use the appropriate idiom to link the two sentences and make one longer sentence.

THE KEY

The key provides answers only to the *Work it out* exercises, where you have to guess the meaning of idioms from example sentences. There are no single correct answers to the other exercises. Get a teacher or native speaker to check your answers.

THE INDEX

The index is an alphabetically-ordered list of all the idioms contained in the material. You can use it to find quickly the meaning or usage of a particular idiom, to revise as you go along and as a record of what you have learned when you finish the book. It collects together the various idioms made with particular verbs, such as *make* and *look*, and cross refers synonymous idioms.

PHRASAL VERBS WITHOUT OBJECTS

Read the introduction on pages 1–4 before you begin work.

■ A phrasal verb = verb + preposition
                   or
             verb + adverbial particle

There are four major types of phrasal verb
A   without an object
B   may be separated by an object (separable)
C   never separated by an object (inseparable)
D   linked to an object by an extra preposition

■ This unit looks at Type A. Phrasal verbs without objects are used in the same way as normal verbs
    I got up at seven o'clock.
    What time did you get up?

■ Some Type A phrasal verbs may also be used with an object
    wake up   *wake (someone) up*
    drop out   *drop out of (something)*

■ Common, self-explanatory phrasal verbs, such as *stand up* and *sit down* are not included.

■ It can be difficult to decide whether a phrasal verb is being used idiomatically or literally
    Man (standing at window): Look out! There's a woman with a gun!
Look out! in this example could mean either 'Look out of the window!' or 'Beware!'

■ Do not confuse verb + particle combinations with ordinary verbs
    take over   take control of
    overtake   pass another vehicle on the road

SECTION 1.1

wake up   also **wake (someone) up**
   regain consciousness after sleeping
   I woke up late this morning.

get up   also **get (someone) up**
   rise (from a bed or reclining position)   ☆
   He gets up at seven o'clock every morning.

grow up
   become adult
   My son wants to be a pilot when he grows up.

slip up
   make a careless mistake
   *I slipped up several times at the interview and
   didn't get the job.*

give up   also **give (something) up**
   abandon one's efforts, stop doing something
   *The crossword puzzle was too difficult, so
   I gave up.*

drop out   also **drop out of (something)**
   withdraw (from a group activity)
   *The course was very difficult and many students
   dropped out.*

stand out   also **stand out from (something)**
   be noticeable
   *That house stands out because it's the only new
   house in the neighbourhood.*

stick out
   protrude   ☆
   *I bought a new case, but a nail was sticking out,
   so I took it back to the shop.*

look out   also **look out for (someone/thing)**
   beware (generally a command)
   Look out! There's a snake behind you.

go out
   be extinguished (a fire, light)   ☆
   Suddenly the lights went out.

Ask and answer

1. What time do you usually get up?
2. What's that sticking out of his pocket?
    (calculator)
3. Why didn't you come to the Spanish
    class this week?
4. Why did the fire go out? (rain)
5. How many people drop out of
    university each year? (2,000)

Complete the sentence

1. (wake up) He missed his train
    because...
2. (grow up) She wants to be a doctor
    when...
3. (slip up) His boss was angry because...
4. (stand out) People always notice her.
    She...
5. (look out) The ice on the road is very
    dangerous, so...

On your own

Make up sentences using these ten idioms.
Use a dictionary to find out the other
meanings of idioms marked ☆.

SECTION 1.2

Ask and answer

1. Did the teacher show up to your last lesson?
2. If you were being chased by a lion, how would you get away?
3. Have you ever turned up at a party without being asked?
4. If you were being threatened, would you back down or fight?
5. If your car breaks down on the motorway, what should you do?

Complete the sentence

1. (back out) He promised to come on a mountaineering expedition with us, but ...
2. (die down) The riots in Liverpool lasted about two days and then ...
3. (settle down) New employees often feel uneasy before ...
4. (die out) If pandas aren't protected, ...
5. (run away) Yesterday a child broke my window and ...

On your own

Make up sentences using these ten idioms. Use a dictionary to find out the other meanings of idioms marked ☆.

break down
> stop functioning (mainly machines)
> *My television broke down, but I managed to repair it myself.*

settle down
> get used to a new situation (a house, job, school)
> *We moved into this house last month, but we still haven't settled down.*

run away   also **run away from (someone/thing)**
> flee
> *The thief ran away when she heard the police siren.*

get away   also **get away from (someone/thing)**
> escape
> *The police chased the thief, but he got away.*

show up
> appear or come as expected   ☆
> *We invited ten guests, but only four showed up.*

turn up
> appear or come unexpectedly   ☆
> *He often turns up at parties without an invitation.*

back out   also **back out from (something)**
> withdraw (from a promise or plan)
> *He promised to help me with my homework, but he backed out when he saw how difficult it was.*

back down
> withdraw (from a threat)
> *The workers threatened to go on strike, but they backed down after a long meeting.*

die out
> become extinct (a species of animal)
> *The brontosaurus died out millions of years ago.*

die down
> diminish and finally disappear (a sound, fire, emotion)
> *The fire blazed all night, and died away slowly in the morning.*

SECTION 1.3

fall through
    fail (plans, arrangements)
    *My plan to go abroad fell through when my
    father refused to lend me any money.*

give in   also **give in to (someone)**
    surrender
    *The soldiers were surrounded by enemy troops,
    but they refused to give in.*

set off   also **set out**
    begin a journey ☆
    *We set off at dawn and reached our destination
    by noon.*

step down   also **step down from (something)**
    retire from a high position
    *The company president stepped down so that
    his position could be occupied by a younger
    person.*

run out   also **run out of (something)**
    become exhausted (supplies, stocks) ☆
    *The soldiers surrendered when their
    ammunition ran out.*

get on   also **get along**
    progress or manage ☆
    He's getting on very well in his new job.

wear out
    become unusable after excessive use (clothes,
    machine parts)
    *My favourite coat finally wore out and I had to
    buy a new one.*

wear off
    gradually disappear (effects, influence, novelty,
    colour)
    *The effects of vaccinations wear off after a few
    hours.*

break out
    begin suddenly (an epidemic, violence) ☆
    An epidemic of flu broke out in rural areas.

break up
    disperse or disband (a group or association of
    people)
    *The crowd broke up as the police started to use
    tear-gas.*

Ask and answer

1. How are you getting on with English idioms?
2. How long does the effect of aspirins take to wear off?
3. What do you do with clothes when they wear out?
4. At what age should politicians step down?
5. What time do you set off in the morning?

Complete the sentence

1. (break up) As soon as the police arrived, the demonstration...
2. (break out) The police were called to the pub because...
3. (fall through) The government refused to support our project, so...
4. (give in) My children kept asking me to take them to the zoo and...
5. (run out) The shipwrecked sailors died when their food supply...

On your own

Make up sentences using these ten idioms. Use a dictionary to find out the other meanings of idioms marked ☆.

SECTION 1.4

Work it out

Try to work out the meanings of the idioms on this page from the example sentences and then write in the definitions. Check the answers in the key at the back of the book or in a dictionary.

On your own

Make up sentences using these ten idioms.

1. **blow up**

   Terrorists left a bomb in the main station and several people were killed when it blew up.

2. **take off**

   Fasten your seat belts, please. The plane is about to take off.

3. **show off**

   John has a very high opinion of himself and he always shows off in front of his friends.

4. **cheer up**

   Mary was depressed, so I took her to see a comic film and she soon cheered up.

5. **calm down**

   The woman was shocked by the accident, but calmed down after drinking a glass of whisky.

6. **dress up**

   I have to dress up tonight because I'm going to a wedding reception.

7. **branch out**

   After a very successful year, our firm decided to branch out and establish offices in other cities.

8. **crop up**

   Whenever financial problems crop up, I ask my bank manager for advice.

9. **pass out**

   The man passed out when he thought he saw a ghost.

10. **come round**   also **come to**

    He came round when his friend threw a bucket of water over him.

2 SEPARABLE PHRASAL VERBS

The phrasal verbs in this unit – called separable phrasal verbs – always have objects. They are used in the same way as normal verbs, except

they may be separated by noun objects

He	put	his coat	on.
	verb	noun object	particle

they must be separated by pronoun objects

He	put	it	on.
	verb	pronoun object	particle

■ They cannot be separated by adverbs
    He put on his coat quickly.
    He quickly put his coat on.

■ Some phrasal verbs can only be used with certain classes of object
    throw (something) away
    call (someone) up

■ Some phrasal verbs have different meanings with different classes of object
    take clothes off   remove, undress
    take people off   imitate, mock

■ It can be difficult to decide when a separable phrasal verb is being used idiomatically and when literally
    She carried her bag out. (literal)
    She carried her plan out. (idiomatic)

■ Some particles are used with a constant meaning.
up often implies completely
    He ate up his dinner.
with *add, break, burn, chew, clean, count, drink, eat, tear, wash*
down often implies to the ground
    They cut the tree down.
with *burn, cut, take, tear*
off often implies removal of one thing from the surface of another
    He washed off the dirt.
with *brush, clean, dust, wash, wipe*

SECTION 2.1

Ask and answer

1. (put on) What do you do when your hands are cold?
2. (pick up) What would you do if you saw some money in the street?
3. (take out) What do you do when a cake in the oven is starting to burn?
4. (throw away) What did you do with last year's calendar?
5. (give up) What would you do if you were too busy to study English?

Complete the sentence

1. (call off) Half the orchestra contracted flu, so the concert . . .
2. (take up) She was bored, so . . .
3. (turn on) He wanted to watch the television news, . . .
4. (turn up) The radio was on very softly, . . .
5. (put off) None of the members could attend the meeting, so . . .

On your own

Make up sentences with these ten idioms. Use a dictionary to find out the other meanings of idioms marked ☆.

put (something) on   opposite **take off**
   dress in (a hat, clothes, shoes) ☆
   She put her coat on and went out.

pick (something) up   opposite **put down**
   grasp and raise ☆
   I picked my pen up and started to write.

take (something) out   opposite **put away**
   remove from (a container, enclosure) ☆
   I took out my books and began to study.

turn (something) on   opposite **turn off**
   start (an electrical appliance) ☆
   It was dark, so I turned the light on.

turn (something) up   opposite **turn down**
   increase the output of (an electrical appliance) ☆
   I can't hear the radio. Please turn it up.

throw (something) away
   discard
   He ate the last biscuit and threw the packet away.

take (something) up
   begin to practise or study ☆
   He took up tennis last year.

give (something) up
   stop (an activity, habit)
   She tried several times to give up smoking, and finally succeeded.

put (something) off
   postpone ☆
   It's raining so hard, we'll have to put our picnic off until tomorrow.

call (something) off
   cancel (a planned activity) ☆
   The lecture was called off because the speaker was ill.

SECTION 2.2

look (something) up
    seek (information) in a reference book
    Always look up the meaning of a new word in
      the dictionary.

find (something) out
    discover or obtain (information)
    How did you find out my address?

make (something) up
    invent (a story)
    He said he once played golf with Winston
      Churchill, but I think he's making it up.

carry (something) out
    perform (a plan, threat)
    He spent his life planning a revolution, but he
      died before he could carry it out.

think (something) over
    consider carefully
    I asked her to help me and she said she would
      think it over.

talk (something) over
    discuss
    You'd better talk your plan over with your
      parents.

work (something) out   also **figure out**
    solve or calculate
    It took me hours to work out how much money
      I owed.

show (something) off
    display with pride
    She walked slowly through the park to show off
      her new hairstyle.

mix (something) up
    confuse
    I mixed up the dates of my interviews and went
      to the wrong place.

sort (something) out
    organise or clarify
    The new clerk spent hours sorting out the files.

Ask and answer

1. (make up) Is his story true?
2. (look up) How can I find out John's telephone number?
3. (show off) Why did she invite us for a drive in her new car?
4. (think over) What would you do if you were offered a new job?
5. (work out) Why does he take a calculator when he goes shopping?

Complete the sentence

1. (mix up) The hotel clerk couldn't find our room number because someone...
2. (carry out) The hijacker threatened to kill the hostages, but...
3. (talk over) Whenever I have a problem,...
4. (sort out) Before the postman can deliver letters,...
5. (find out) He called the Airport Information Office...

On your own

Make up sentences using these ten idioms.

SECTION 2.3

Ask and answer

1. (bring up) What's the main role of a parent?
2. (let down) Why is she angry with her friend?
3. (see off) Why did Mike go to the station?
4. (take on) What does a company do when an employee retires or leaves?
5. (call up) What do you do when you want to speak to someone urgently?

Complete the sentence

1. (back up) When a teacher wants to punish students, the principal always...
2. (give away) A student stole some money, but the caretaker...
3. (bring round) My father fainted on the bus, and the conductor...
4. (knock out) A rock fell on the climber's head and...
5. (put off) I never listen to records while I'm doing my homework because...

On your own

Make up sentences using these ten idioms. Use a dictionary to find out the other meanings of idioms marked ☆.

call (someone) up
telephone ☆
My friend called me up last night for a chat.

see (someone) off
accompany someone to his/her point of departure
They came to the airport to see us off.

back (someone) up
give support to
No one backed me up in my dispute with the local council.

let (someone) down
disappoint (by failing to act as expected/promised)
She promised to help me, but then she let me down.

bring (someone) up
raise (a child)
His parents died when he was young and he was brought up by his uncle.

bring (someone) round
revive ☆
A passenger fainted but the stewardess brought him round.

knock (someone) out
make unconscious by hitting ☆
The boxing champion knocked the challenger out in the first round.

put (someone) off
distract ☆
The baby's screams put me off and I couldn't finish my homework.

give (someone) away
betray ☆
He pretended to be English, but his faint Greek accent gave him away.

take (someone) on   opposite **lay (someone) off**
give employment to ☆
Our company is taking on ten new employees next month.

SECTION 2.4

1. **take (something) down**

   The policeman took down what the thief said and later showed his report to the judge.

2. **cross (something) out**

   I crossed out the spelling mistake and wrote the correct spelling above it.

3. **try (something) on**

   I tried six jackets on in the shop before deciding which one to buy.

4. **draw (something) up**

   When the negotiations had finished, our lawyers drew up the contract.

5. **fill (something) out**

   The customs officer handed me a declaration form and asked me to fill it out.

6. **hand (something) out**

   The teacher handed out the test papers before the test and collected them again at the end.

7. **take (something) back**

   I'm sorry I made that rude remark. I take it back.

8. **bring (something) up**

   I was worried about our financial position, so I brought the matter up at the meeting.

9. **break (something) in**

   New shoes are usually stiff and uncomfortable until they have been broken in.

10. **buy (something) up**

    He bought up the complete stock of spare parts.

Work it out

Try to work out the meanings of the idioms on this page from the example sentences and then write in the definitions. Check your answers in the key at the back of the book or in a dictionary.

On your own

Make up sentences using these ten idioms.

3 INSEPARABLE PHRASAL VERBS

The phrasal verbs in this unit – called inseparable phrasal verbs – always have objects, but they can never be separated by them. They are sometimes separated by adverbs
I looked everywhere for my book.

■ They are used in the same way as normal verbs.

■ It can be difficult to decide when an inseparable phrasal verb is used idiomatically and when literally
The police are looking into the robbery.
The police are looking into the bank.
In the first example *looking into* means 'investigating', and in the second example it is used literally.

SECTION 3.1

call on (someone)
    visit ☆
    *My sister called on me yesterday because I was
    ill.*

call for (someone/something)
    come to collect ☆
    *I'm leaving my car at the garage and will call for
    it tomorrow.*

get on (something)   opposite **get off**
    board or enter (a train, bus)
    *He got on the bus at Waterloo and got off at
    Piccadilly.*

get into (something)   opposite **get out of**
    enter (a small, enclosed space like a car, bath) ☆
    The door closed as we were getting into the lift.

look for (someone/something)
    seek
    He looked everywhere for his door key.

get over (something)
    recover from (shock, disappointment, illness)
    He never got over the death of his father.

look after (someone/something)
    take care of
    *I hired a babysitter to look after my children
    when I went to the theatre.*

count on (someone/something)
    rely on
    I am counting on you to help me tomorrow.

do without (someone/something)
    manage without or abstain from
    *I'll have to do without my car while it's being
    repaired.*

look into (something)
    investigate
    The police are looking into last night's robbery.

Ask and answer

1. (call for) Shall I meet you at the cinema? No, ...
2. (look into) Do the police know how the fire started? No, ...
3. (get over) Is she still upset about failing her exam? No, ...
4. (get on) What did you do when the bus came? I ...
5. (look for) What did you do when you lost your wallet? I ...

Complete the sentence

1. (call on) Yesterday a door-to-door salesman ...
2. (get into) The telephone rang just as I ...
3. (count on) The weather forecast said it would be fine, but you shouldn't ...
4. (do without) My father is addicted to cigarettes. He can't ...
5. (look after) While we were on holiday, our neighbours ...

On your own

Make up sentences using these ten idioms. Use a dictionary to find out the other meanings of idioms marked ☆.

SECTION 3.2

Ask and answer

1. How did you come by this textbook?
2. Who waits on customers in a self-service restaurant?
3. What does UFO stand for?
4. What type of goods do grocers deal in?
5. Have you ever fallen for a card trick?

Complete the sentence

1. (see through) He tried to sell me a worthless painting, but...
2. (go over) I discovered several mistakes when I...
3. (account for) My brother's got a headache, which...
4. (come across) Looking through a pile of old books, I...
5. (deal with) The complaints department will...

On your own

Make up sentences using these ten idioms. Use a dictionary to find out the other meanings of idioms marked ☆.

stand for (something)
represent (usually an abbreviation) ☆
UNO stands for the United Nations Organisation.

deal with (something)
treat (a topic) or tackle (a problem) ☆
I'll deal with your question after the meeting.

deal in (something)
sell (as a business activity)
This company deals in foreign cars.

come by (something)
acquire
How did you come by that rare stamp?

come across (someone/thing) also **come upon**
meet or find by chance
As I was walking along the beach, I came across an old silver coin.

go over (something)
review
Let's go over the structures we studied last week.

account for (something)
explain the cause of
He missed his train, which accounts for his late arrival.

fall for (something)
be deceived by (a trick) ☆
A market trader told me this ring was made of gold and I fell for it.

see through (something)
notice deception
I saw through the salesman's trick and refused to buy his goods.

wait on (someone)
serve (food and drink) to
She gave up her job as a stewardess because she was tired of waiting on rude passengers.

SECTION 3.3

go with (something)
> match or suit (other articles of clothing)
> *That shirt goes well with those trousers.*

break into (something)
> enter by force
> *A burglar broke into my house while I was on holiday.*

live on (something)
> eat or drink only certain things
> *When I was in the Bahamas, I lived on water melons.*

take after (someone)
> resemble in character or appearance an older relative
> *John takes after his father, although his hair is much darker.*

hear from (someone)
> receive (a letter, telephone call) from someone
> *I haven't heard from him since he went abroad.*

hear of (someone/something)
> hear or read about ☆
> *Have you ever heard of the Kon Tiki expedition?*

get round (something)
> evade or solve (a problem)
> *He couldn't pay his rent, but he got round it by borrowing some money.*

count against (someone)
> act/be used as an obstacle in achieving something
> *His lack of practice counted against him in the tennis tournament.*

believe in (someone/something)
> have faith in someone; have faith in the existence or validity of something.
> *My sister believes strongly in astrology.*

go through (something)
> experience (an ordeal)
> *She went through terrible post-natal depression.*

Ask and answer

1. Which of your parents do you take after most?
2. Have you ever heard of Patagonia?
3. Do you believe in ghosts?
4. Would green striped trousers go well with a purple shirt?
5. If your door was locked and you couldn't find the key, how would you get round the problem?

Complete the sentence

1. (break into) That man was arrested because...
2. (count against) A bad qualification is sometimes worse than no qualification because...
3. (go through) The refugees had...
4. (hear from) I know George is still living in China because...
5. (live on) The shipwrecked sailors stayed alive by ...

On your own

Make up sentences using these ten idioms. Use a dictionary to find out the other meanings of idioms marked ☆.

SECTION 3.4

Work it out

Try to work out the meanings of the idioms on this page from the example sentences and then write in the definitions. Check your answers in the key at the back of the book or in a dictionary.

On your own

Make up sentences using these ten idioms.

1. **keep on**

   The teacher was angry with the student because he kept on arriving late.

2. **carry on**

   Even though the students had fallen asleep, the teacher carried on talking.

3. **go on**

   A fight broke out in the club, but the band went on playing.

4. **burst out**

   When I told her about her father's death, she burst out crying.

5. **feel like**

   I don't feel like studying today. Let's go to the cinema instead.

6. **go for**

   I don't like this design, but I certainly go for that one.

7. **come into**

   He came into a small fortune when his uncle died, but six months later he was penniless again.

8. **long for**

   When I'm sitting in this hot office, I long for a glass of cold beer.

9. **get through**

   We got through the whole textbook in three months.

10. **frown on**

    My father hasn't forbidden me to ride a motorbike, but he frowns on it.

4 PHRASAL VERBS WITH EXTRA PREPOSITIONS

Many of the idioms in this unit are derived from Type A phrasal verbs (see Unit 1).

Type A

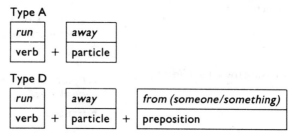

Some Type D phrasal verbs resemble Type A idioms, but are not related in meaning

Type A   *get up*   rise (from a bed, sofa etc.)
Type D   *get up to (something)*   do (mischief)

■ Most of these idioms cannot be separated by objects
   We're looking forward to our holiday.
but they may be separated by adverbs
   I look back with regret on my past life.

■ A few Type D phrasal verbs can be separated by an object, for example
   take (someone) up on (something)
but these are uncommon and are not included here.

SECTION 4.1

Ask and answer

1. (fall out with) Why didn't Peter and Julie get married?
2. (get along with) Why did Mike give up his job at the bookshop?
3. (carry on with) What did the band do when the fire started?
4. (do away with) What would you do if you had political power?
5. (get on with) What did the manager say to the talkative employee?

Complete the sentence

1. (put up with) She stopped working at the glue factory because...
2. (get away with) John played a practical joke on his teacher, but...
3. (keep up with) He runs very fast. Nobody...
4. (go through with) They planned to cross the North Pole, but...
5. (catch up with) I chased the bus on my bicycle, but...

On your own

Make up sentences using these ten idioms. Use a dictionary to find the other meanings of idioms marked ☆.

get along with (someone)   also **get on with**
　have a good relationship with
　I get along well with my boss.

fall out with (someone)
　quarrel with
　They fell out with each other over what type of car to buy.

catch up with (someone/something)
　follow and reach by travelling faster   ☆
　We chased the enemy troops and caught up with them at the river.

keep up with (someone/something)
　travel at the same speed as a moving person or thing   ☆
　Please walk more slowly. I can't keep up with you.

put up with (someone/something)
　tolerate
　I stopped living with Michael because I couldn't put up with his terrible jokes.

get away with (something)
　do something which normally incurs punishment, but go unpunished
　He got away with killing his wife by making it look like an accident.

go through with (something)
　perform a difficult act as planned
　He says he'll climb Mount Everest, but I doubt if he'll go through with it.

carry on with (something)
　continue doing
　He carried on with his work, in spite of the noise outside.

get on with (something)
　resume doing   ☆
　Excuse me, but I must get on with my homework.

do away with (something)
　abolish
　The headmaster thinks school uniforms should be done away with.

SECTION 4.2

make up for (something)
    compensate for
    The employee made up for his late arrival by
      working overtime.

run out of (something)
    exhaust supplies of
    We ran out of petrol just after we joined the
      motorway.

look forward to (something)
    anticipate with pleasure
    I'm looking forward to my trip to Holland.

look back on (something)
    recall
    I look back on my schooldays with little
      pleasure.

look up to (someone)
    respect
    I look up to great politicians, but I don't envy
      them.

stand up for (someone/something)
    defend verbally
    When they criticised my father, I stood up for
      him.

stand up to (someone)
    resist (an intimidating person)
    I stood up to my interrogators for as long as I
      could, and refused to answer their questions.

face up to (someone/something)
    confront (a person, problem)
    I don't have the courage to face up to my boss
      and ask for a rise.

get out of (something)
    avoid having to fulfil (an obligation) ☆
    He was supposed to take an exam, but he got
      out of it by pretending to be ill.

get down to (something)
    begin to make a serious effort
    Making shelves sounded difficult, but once I got
      down to it, I found it easy.

Ask and answer

1. (face up to) What did he do when he had a problem?
2. (run out of) What is the biggest danger for anyone travelling across a wide desert?
3. (stand up for) What would you do if someone criticised your mother?
4. (look back on) How do you feel about your childhood?
5. (stand up to) What did the staff do when the management tried to cut their wages?

Complete the sentence

1. (look up to) My father is very honest, so . . .
2. (look forward to) Thank you for your invitation. I . . .
3. (make up for) I broke my friend's camera, but . . .
4. (get down to) I went to the beach yesterday, instead of . . .
5. (get out of) My mother wanted me to go shopping, but I . . .

On your own

Make up sentences using these ten idioms. Use a dictionary to find the other meanings of idioms marked ☆.

SECTION 4.3

Ask and answer

1. Has your life so far lived up to your expectations?
2. Have you ever come down with a serious illness?
3. If you wanted to lose weight, what would you cut down on?
4. What is the minimum amount of sleep you can get by with?
5. Do you ever wait up for members of your family?

Complete the sentence

1. (come up with) I considered the problem carefully and finally...
2. (grow out of) My son suffers from asthma, but his doctor says...
3. (hold on to) The monkey grabbed my camera, but...
4. (fall back on) I hope there's enough food for everyone, but we can always...
5. (check up on) In order to find out how drugs were smuggled into the country, the police...

On your own

Make up sentences using these ten idioms.

live up to (something)
fulfil (expectations) or justify (a reputation)
The hotel lived up to our expectations.

wait up for (someone/something)
not go to bed until someone arrives/something happens
When I arrived home at two in the morning, Jean was still waiting up for me.

hold on to (someone/thing) opposite **let go of**
grasp
If you don't hold on to the string, your kite will blow away.

grow out of (something)
be cured of as a result of growing older
He used to stammer, but he grew out of it.

come up with (something)
conceive (an idea, solution)
The economic advisers came up with a plan to counter inflation.

come down with (something)
suddenly fall ill with
My brother has just come down with influenza.

cut down on (something)
reduce one's consumption of
My doctor told me to cut down on cigarettes.

fall back on (someone/something)
use when other resources have been exhausted
After spending all his wages, he fell back on his savings.

get by with (something)
manage or survive (with a minimum of)
I get by with a little help from my friends.

check up on (someone/something)
investigate
The tax office is checking up on our accounts.

SECTION 4.4

1. **walk out on (someone)**

   *She walked out on her husband when she
   realised she didn't love him anymore.*

2. **turn out for (something)**

   *Thousands of people turned out for the
   meeting, despite the pouring rain.*

3. **run away with**

   *He should be stopped before his desire for
   power runs away with him.*

4. **look out for**

   Look out for fresh pasta while you're in Italy.

5. **keep away from**

   *I'm always telling him to keep away from that
   dog, but he won't listen. One day he'll get
   bitten.*

6. **break in on**

   *John and Mike were talking on the phone, when
   suddenly a third voice broke in on their
   conversation.*

7. **catch up on**

   *After spending two years abroad, there's a lot
   of news to catch up on.*

8. **look down on**

   *Mr Jones is a terrible snob and has always
   looked down on anyone with a lower income
   than him.*

9. **latch on to**

   *Once she's latched on to an idea, she can't talk
   about anything else.*

10. **get up to**

    *What have you been getting up to while I've
    been away?*

Work it out

Try to work out the meanings of the
idioms on this page from the example
sentences and then write in the definitions.
Check your answers in the key at the back
of the book or in a dictionary.

On your own

Make up sentences using these ten idioms.

5 VERB-NOUN COMBINATIONS

The verbs *take* and *make* are used idiomatically with many different objects. The meaning is usually clear from the context, and the important thing is to remember the correct verb.

take a bath, a bus, an examination, a holiday, a message,
an opportunity, a photograph, a risk, a seat, a shower, a test,
a train, a trip, a vacation, a walk
breakfast, care, dinner, lunch, medicine

make an appointment, an attempt, a bet, a comment, a complaint,
an effort, an error, a loss, a mistake, a noise, a plan, a prediction,
a profit, a promise, a proposal, a remark, a request, a speech,
a statement, a suggestion
progress, haste

■ In some verb-noun combinations, the verb is surprising
catch a cold
pay a compliment

■ It can be difficult to decide when a verb-noun combination is being used idiomatically or literally. For example *make a bed* means 'prepare for use' (idiomatic) and 'build' (literal).

■ In some verb-noun combinations, both verb and noun are used idiomatically
take heart
lose heart

■ Nouns used idiomatically in verb-noun combinations often have a plural as well as singular form
run an errand
run errands

■ The idioms in Section 5.1 are easy to understand from the context and therefore are given without definitions.

SECTION 5.1

catch a cold (or other infectious disease)
He played golf in the rain and caught a cold.

keep a secret
Tell me where you're going for your honeymoon. I can keep a secret.

set an example
The managing director tried to set an example to the company employees by arriving on time in the morning.

hold a meeting (or other arranged gathering)
The union is holding a meeting to discuss the wage claim.

drop a hint
He dropped several hints about the time, but his guests still didn't leave.

run an errand
Paul often runs errands for his mother, like posting letters and buying groceries.

open an account opposite **close an account**
I opened a post office savings account and closed my bank account.

make a living also **earn a living**
He used to be a teacher, but now he makes a living selling cars.

tell the time
My daughter's just learning to tell the time.

kill time
I had nothing to do until the boat left at six, so I went to the cinema to kill time.

Ask and answer

1. Do you ever run errands for anyone?
2. What do you do to kill time?
3. Have you ever caught an infectious disease?
4. Can you keep secrets from your parents?
5. At what age did you learn to tell the time?

Complete the sentence

1. (meeting) We need to discuss this matter. Shall we . . . ?
2. (example) Parents who smoke . . .
3. (account) I wanted to save money, so . . .
4. (hint) My boss didn't tell me to work harder, but . . .
5. (living) What do you do . . . ?

On your own

Make up sentences using these ten idioms.

SECTION 5.2

Ask and answer

1. (the music) What should you do if your careless behaviour causes an accident?
2. (the sack) What might happen to a lazy worker?
3. (face) What happens when a teacher makes a mistake?
4. (a fuss) What would you do if you were overcharged in a restaurant?
5. (the buck) What do people do in order to avoid making difficult decisions?

Complete the sentence

1. (a blank) I visited several companies in search of a job, but...
2. (heart) I expected to fail my driving test, but when the examiner smiled I...
3. (a scene) I'll get off this train at the next station if you...
4. (place) According to today's newspaper, a robbery...
5. (sense) Your explanation is very confusing. It doesn't...

On your own

Make up sentences using these ten idioms.

take place
happen
An accident took place in the High Street today.

take heart   opposite **lose heart**
be encouraged
He had been unemployed for several months, but when he saw the perfect job advertised, he took heart.

lose face   opposite **gain face**
suffer loss of reputation (as a result of some incident)
Several people lost face over the sudden change of policy.

make a scene
create an embarrassing situation by displaying emotion
He made a scene in the pub because his girlfriend was drinking too much.

make a fuss
complain
I wasn't satisfied with my hotel room, so I made a fuss.

draw a blank
fail to get results
The police questioned several suspects, but they drew a blank.

face the music
meet the consequences (bad) of some action
The company president flew to Hawaii with the shareholders' money, and left the managing director to face the music.

pass the buck
transfer responsibility (to someone else)
The sergeant made a false arrest and tried to pass the buck to a subordinate.

get the sack   also **give (someone) the sack**
be dismissed
Joe was always late for work and finally he got the sack.

make sense
be intelligible
Your sentences are too long and they don't make sense.

SECTION 5.3

keep (one's) temper   opposite **lose (one's) temper**
> not get angry
> *It's difficult to keep your temper when people criticise you unfairly.*

keep (one's) head   opposite **lose (one's) head**
> remain calm
> *When the ship started to sink, the crew panicked and only the captain kept his head.*

keep (one's) word   opposite **break (one's) word**
> fulfil a promise
> *You can't rely on Philip because he never keeps his word.*

lose (one's) touch
> be unable to do something as well as before
> *He used to be good at tennis, but recently he's lost his touch.*

change (one's) tune
> change one's stated opinion or attitude
> *He said he didn't like cars, but he changed his tune when I offered him a lift home.*

take (one's) time
> act without haste
> *I always take my time when buying new shoes.*

make (one's) point
> present opinions convincingly
> *He was a passionate believer in peaceful revolution and always made his point strongly.*

learn (one's) lesson
> reform after experiencing the consequences of mistakes
> *He learned his lesson after losing his licence for drinking and driving.*

show (one's) face
> appear in public
> *After his foolish behaviour at the club, he didn't dare to show his face there again.*

do (one's) best
> try as hard as possible
> *I shall do my best to pass the examination.*

Ask and answer

1. If your house caught fire, would you panic? No, ...
2. Do you ever break your promises? No, ...
3. Do you usually order meals in a hurry? No, ...
4. When people are rude to you, do you always get angry? No, ...
5. Can you argue about things convincingly? Yes, ...

Complete the sentence

1. (faces) The manager told us to get out of his restaurant and never ...
2. (touch) Susan was a good pianist when she was young, but now ...
3. (tune) He used to be anti-union, but when he joined this company, he ...
4. (lesson) I used to smoke in bed, but when my bed caught fire, I ...
5. (best) When I asked the mechanic to repair my car, he said ...

On your own

Make up sentences using these ten idioms.

SECTION 5.4

Work it out

Try to work out the meanings of the idioms on this page from the example sentences and then write in the definitions. Check your answers in the key at the back of the book or in a dictionary.

On your own

Make up sentences using these ten idioms.

1. **slip (one's) mind**

   She asked me to post a letter for her, but it completely slipped my mind.

2. **change (one's) mind**

   I ordered steak, but then I changed my mind and asked the waiter to bring me fish instead.

3. **make up (one's) mind**

   I can't make up my mind whether to spend my holiday in Greece or Italy.

4. **speak (one's) mind**

   George is very frank and always speaks his mind even if it upsets people.

5. **lose (one's) mind**

   When she stepped into the cupboard and shut the door, we thought she had lost her mind.

6. **pull (one's) weight**

   My boss warned me that if I didn't pull my weight, I would be dismissed.

7. **eat (one's) words**

   My father said that I played the piano very badly, but when I won the school piano competition, he had to eat his words.

8. **serve (one's) needs**

   This car isn't exactly what I wanted, but it will serve my needs.

9. **make (one's) mark**

   Messner made his mark in mountaineering when he climbed Mount Everest without oxygen tanks.

10. **rack (one's) brains**

    Whenever I have a problem, I always sit down and rack my brains until I think of a solution.

6 VERB-NOUN-PREPOSITION COMBINATIONS

The idioms in this unit take an object
  set fire to (something)
  take pity on (someone)

■ In most of these idioms the noun keeps its literal meaning and only the verb and preposition are used idiomatically
  play tricks on (someone)
  take pride in (something)
but occasionally the noun is used idiomatically
  give rise to (something)
  take exception to (someone/something)

■ All the idioms presented in this unit are invariable, except
  play a trick/tricks on, have an effect/effects on, bear the cost/costs of, bear a grudge/grudges against

■ Some verb-noun-preposition combinations are very similar to verb-noun combinations, but have a completely different meaning
  take care   be careful
  take care of   look after

SECTION 6.1

Ask and answer

1. (fire) What do arsonists do?
2. (trick) Why was the teacher angry with her students?
3. (advantage) What might happen if you left your house unlocked?
4. (attention) What must you do when driving?
5. (part) What do the delegates do at a conference?

Complete the sentence

1. (sight) As I was walking through the jungle, I...
2. (friends) When I was a student, I...
3. (effect) His father's death...
4. (fun) She is very thin and her friends...
5. (fault) My mother always...

On your own

Make up sentences using these ten idioms.

find fault with (someone/something)
  criticise
  My teacher always finds fault with me and with my work.

make fun of (someone/thing)   also **poke fun at**
  mock or tease
  His classmates often made fun of him because his ears stuck out.

play a trick on (someone)   also **play a joke on**
  trick
  My children often play tricks on me, like hiding my spectacles and putting spiders in my shoes.

take advantage of (someone/something)
  exploit
  I'm willing to help you, but don't try to take advantage of me.

have an effect on (someone/something)
  affect
  The film had a big effect on me and afterwards I felt very depressed.

pay attention to (someone/something)
  look at, listen to or think about carefully
  Students should pay attention to what their teacher says.

take part in (something)
  participate in
  Sixteen drivers took part in the Grand Prix.

make friends with (someone)   also **be friends with**
  become friendly with
  I soon made friends with my new neighbours by asking them to our party.

set fire to (something)
  ignite
  The day after the man was released from prison, he set fire to a bus.

catch sight of (someone/something)
  notice
  As he was talking to the suspect, the policeman caught sight of a bloodstain on her sleeve.

SECTION 6.2

make amends to (someone) for (something)
compensate
I made amends to my colleagues for arriving late by buying them all a drink.

make way for (someone)
allow to pass
The reporters made way for the President.

give way to (someone)
yield to ☆
I never give way to my children when they want me to buy them sweets.

give birth to (someone)
bear (a baby)
Our dog gave birth to five puppies in a shoe-box in the garage.

draw the line at (something)
refuse to do or permit
I allow my daughter to stay up late, but I draw the line at all-night parties.

draw a distinction between (someone/thing) and (someone/thing)
distinguish between
I always draw a distinction between intentional and unintentional acts.

bear a grudge against (someone/something)
resent
My neighbours have borne a grudge against their former employer ever since they were made redundant.

bear the cost of (something)
pay for
The company will bear the cost of your business trip to Japan.

keep company with (someone)
associate with
I don't allow my children to keep company with delinquents.

keep watch over (something)
guard or protect
The security guards kept watch over the valuable paintings in the gallery.

Ask and answer

1. Do you think parents should sometimes give way to their children?
2. Who is bearing the cost of your education?
3. If you crashed someone else's car, how would you make amends to them?
4. How many children did your mother give birth to?
5. Do you bear a grudge against anyone?

Complete the sentence

1. (company) My mother knows a lot about politics because ...
2. (line) I allow my children to keep rabbits and canaries, but ...
3. (way) The ambulance arrived soon after the accident and the onlookers ...
4. (watch) Some of the patients are very ill, and the nurse ...
5. (distinction) Hijackers and kidnappers receive different penalties because the law ...

On your own

Make up sentences using these ten idioms. Use a dictionary to find the other meanings of idioms marked ☆.

SECTION 6.3

Ask and answer

1. Which sports do you take an interest in?
2. How do you keep in touch with your old school friends?
3. Who put an end to slavery in the USA?
4. How do you get rid of old magazines and newspapers?
5. What did the invention of the telephone give rise to?

Complete the sentence

1. (track) Fashions change so fast that . . .
2. (go) The bird flew away as soon as I . . .
3. (most) This sunny weather may not last for long, so let's . . .
4. (do) Until I have enough money to buy some new shoes, . . .
5. (better) He won the tennis tournament after . . .

On your own

Make up sentences using these ten idioms.

get rid of (someone/something)
dispose of
Some people get rid of old prams and bicycles by throwing them in the river.

make do with (someone/something)
manage with
We can't afford to buy a new car, so we must make do with the one we have.

let go of (someone/thing)   opposite **hold on to**
release from one's grasp
Don't let go of the dog's lead, or it'll run into the road.

give rise to (something)
cause to happen
Stevenson's invention of the steam locomotive gave rise to a revolution in transport.

keep track of (someone/something)
opposite **lose track of**
remain informed about
A sales manager must keep track of market developments in his field.

lose touch with (someone)   opposite **keep in touch with**
be unable to contact
I lost touch with John after he changed his job and moved to London.

take an interest in (someone/something)
be interested in
Teachers often take an interest in their students' problems.

put an end to (something)
stop or abolish
Lord Shaftesbury put an end to the practice of employing women in coal-mines.

make the most of (something)
get maximum advantage from
I've only got two weeks holiday and I intend to make the most of it.

get the better of (someone)
beat
In the last chess tournament, the British champion got the better of his opponent.

SECTION 6.4

1. **take charge of (someone/something)**

   After staging a 'coup d'etat', the armed forces took charge of the country.

2. **take offence at (something)**   also **take exception to**

   My boss took offence at my suggestion that she had made a mistake.

3. **take care of (someone/something)**

   The doctors and nurses took good care of me while I was in hospital.

4. **take pity on (someone)**

   My brother was so poor for a while, that I took pity on him and gave him some money.

5. **take credit for (something)**

   The producer should take credit for the success of that play.

6. **take account of (something)**

   Before choosing a new job, you should take account of the salary and the working hours among other things.

7. **take pride in (something)**

   Bill is a good mechanic because he takes pride in his work.

8. **take revenge on (someone)**

   Henry pushed me into the pond yesterday, but I took revenge on him this morning by breaking an egg over his head.

9. **take a look at (someone/something)**

   After the accident, the policeman took a look at the tyres on all the cars involved.

10. **take hold of (someone/something)**

    He took hold of the rope and started to climb it.

Work it out

Try to work out the meanings of the idioms on this page from the example sentences and then write in the definitions. Check your answers in the key at the back of the book or in a dictionary.

On your own

Make up sentences using these ten idioms.

7 PREPOSITION-NOUN COMBINATIONS

This unit presents idioms where only the preposition is used idiomatically. The meaning of most of these idioms is clear from the context, and the most important thing is to remember the correct preposition
> *in a hurry*
> *on vacation*

■ There are, however, some expressions of this type where the meaning is not obvious, and the most common of these are also presented
> *on purpose*
> *in case*

■ These idioms generally have no plural form (with the exception of *at times* which has no singular form)
> *His parents are very kind at heart.*

■ In some cases other parts of speech are used as nouns
> *in general*
> *at best*

■ The preposition *by* is used with reflexive pronouns to mean 'alone' or 'without help'
> *I live by myself.*

■ The idioms in Section 7.1 are easy to understand from the context and therefore are given without definitions.

SECTION 7.1

in cash
> Will you pay for this car in cash or by cheque?

under consideration
> Your proposal is still under consideration, but we'll let you know when we've made a decision.

at fault
> After the accident, the driver admitted he was at fault.

on fire
> My house is on fire. Please call the fire brigade.

by hand
> This watch was made by hand in Switzerland.

in person
> I've seen the Queen on television many times, but I've never seen her in person.

on schedule
> The train arrived late, but left on schedule.

on strike
> The factory was closed for six weeks when the workers were on strike.

on television
> I watched a good film on television last night.

in theory
> His ideas are very good in theory, but they never work in practice.

Ask and answer

1. (fire) Why did he throw the frying pan through the window?
2. (cash) How would you like to pay for this furniture?
3. (strike) Why are all the trains cancelled today?
4. (schedule) Why did the concert end twenty minutes late?
5. (hand) Is this jumper machine-made?

Complete the sentence

1. (television) I watched a play ...
2. (consideration) The scheme for a new motorway was ...
3. (theory) Her design for a petrol-free car was brilliant ...
4. (fault) The managing director was ...
5. (person) The president refused to appear ...

On your own

Make up sentences using these ten idioms.

SECTION 7.2

Ask and answer

1. (case) Why are you wearing your raincoat?
2. (trial) Why haven't you paid for your new vacuum cleaner yet?
3. (principle) Why does he never work on Sundays?
4. (purpose) Why was the worker who broke his machine dismissed?
5. (vain) Were your efforts to pass the exam successful?

Complete the sentence

1. (fact) He says he is single, but...
2. (board) The ship will leave as soon as...
3. (time) The teacher is never early or late. He always...
4. (time) The driver saw the child run into the road and managed to...
5. (public) Do you enjoy speaking...?

On your own

Make up sentences using these ten idioms. Use a dictionary to find other meanings of idioms marked ☆.

on purpose   opposite **by accident**
　　deliberately
　　I'm sure that dreadful child broke my window on purpose.

on principle
　　because of moral or religious convictions
　　I refuse to join the army on principle.

on trial
　　to be kept only if satisfactory (goods, employees)
　　We took this refrigerator on trial for a week, but we've decided not to buy it.

on board
　　on a ship or plane
　　The ship sails at noon, but all passengers should be on board by eleven o'clock.

on time
　　punctually
　　This train always leaves on time.

in time
　　at or before the critical time ☆
　　I arrived at the station just in time.

in case
　　as a precaution
　　You'd better take your umbrella in case it rains.

in vain
　　without desired results or effects
　　His efforts to pass his driving test were in vain.

in fact
　　actually
　　He pretends to be rich, but in fact he's quite poor.

in public   opposite **in private**
　　publicly, openly
　　She was kind to her dog in public, but was very cruel to it in private.

SECTION 7.3

at heart
according to one's true character
He seems very hard, but he's actually quite kind at heart.

at the moment   also **at present**
now
The manager is busy at the moment. Please come back later.

for certain   also **for sure**
certainly
If you jump out of an aeroplane without a parachute, you'll die for certain.

for a change
contrary to usual behaviour or custom
My teacher gave me a good report, for a change.

by chance
unintentionally or unexpectedly
I had been trying to contact her for months, when I met her by chance at a party.

without fail   also **at all costs**
for certain, regardless of difficulty
You must return my money next Friday without fail.

within reason
subject to reasonable limits
I will do anything you ask within reason.

at times
occasionally
I disagree with my boss at times.

on the contrary
contradicting what has been said
He told me I looked ill, but on the contrary, I felt very well indeed.

to some extent
partly
I agree with you to some extent.

Ask and answer

1. (contrary) Do you find languages easy to learn?
2. (moment) What are you studying?
3. (change) Did he go straight home after work as usual?
4. (heart) Is Mary as charming as she seems to be?
5. (certain) Will you be staying in this country or going abroad for your next holiday?

Complete the sentence

1. (extent) I agree with the government's policies ...
2. (fail) I promise to deliver the goods this month ...
3. (reason) He is willing to do any job ...
4. (times) Mike is usually polite, but ...
5. (chance) Newton discovered gravity ...

On your own

Make up sentences using these ten idioms.

SECTION 7.4

Work it out

Try to work out the meanings of the idioms on this page from the example sentences and then write in the definitions. Check your answers in the key at the back of the book or in a dictionary.

On your own

Make up sentences using these ten idioms.

1. **out of practice**

   He lost the tennis match because he was out of practice.

2. **out of condition**

   I used to be able to run fast, but now I'm out of condition.

3. **out of breath**

   When the messenger arrived, he was out of breath after running so far.

4. **out of work**

   Millions of people are out of work because of the economic recession.

5. **out of fashion**

   Miniskirts were popular for a few years, but when my sister finally bought one, they were out of fashion.

6. **out of season**

   I love strawberries, but they're out of season most of the year.

7. **out of character**

   Mr Clark is normally so quiet that everyone thought his fit of anger was completely out of character.

8. **out of print**

   The bookshop couldn't order the book I wanted because it was out of print.

9. **out of sight**

   I watched the ship until it was out of sight.

10. **out of place**

    I never drink alcohol so I always feel out of place at cocktail parties.

8 PREPOSITION-NOUN AND PREPOSITION-ADJECTIVE-NOUN COMBINATIONS

In Unit 7 only the preposition was used idiomatically. In this unit, the noun is generally used idiomatically.

of course
on edge

■ Most of these idioms are invariable
The students learned the idioms by heart.

■ Sections 8.1 and 8.2 present preposition-noun combinations, and Section 8.3 presents ten preposition-adjective-noun combinations.

SECTION 8.1

Ask and answer

(of course, on edge, by heart, at best, at length)

1. Did a ship ever arrive to save the shipwrecked sailors?
2. Why did the witness sound as if he was reading his answers in court?
3. Did the witness look relaxed while he was being cross-examined?
4. Do you expect the company to do well this year?
5. If a person collapsed in the street, would you stop to help?

Complete the sentence

1. (hand) The accident took place near a hospital, so a doctor...
2. (force) The new law has been approved by parliament and will soon...
3. (effect) A ban on imported animal skins will raise their prices...
4. (way) Production of the new car will soon...
5. (board) After their investigation of the company, the police decided...

On your own

Make up sentences using these ten idioms. Use a dictionary to find the other meanings of idioms marked ☆.

of course
> naturally, certainly
> *Of course I want to learn English.*

on edge
> tense or irritable
> *She's on edge because she hasn't had news of her father's expedition to the Himalayas for two weeks now.*

at length   also **at last**
> eventually
> *I kept on looking for a suitable job and at length I found one.*

by heart
> thoroughly
> *Please learn all these idioms by heart.*

at hand
> readily accessible
> *George can't move around much any more, but he always has his walking sticks at hand.*

under way
> proceeding
> *Construction of the new office building is now under way.*

above board
> honest, legal
> *The activities of this agency are completely above board.*

in effect
> considering the practical implications ☆
> *The new Nationality Law says in effect that people born outside the country will not have a right to citizenship.*

in force
> have legal effect
> *The new police powers have only been in force for six months, but they have already caused a decline in the number of burglaries.*

at best
> in the best possible situation
> *We can expect at best a loss of two million pounds this year.*

SECTION 8.2

on the whole
overall, generally
There are a few mistakes, but on the whole your essay is quite good.

on the run
fleeing from pursuers
He has been on the run ever since the police discovered his hideout.

by the way
incidentally (changing the subject)
I met John last week. By the way, did you know his wife was a professional artist?

off the record
unofficial and not to be reported
The ambassador's comments about the government were strictly off the record.

beside the point
irrelevant
I am a conscientious worker. What I do in my spare time is completely beside the point.

in the balance
remaining uncertain
The judge's decision is still in the balance.

behind the times
old-fashioned
My father's really behind the times – he expects to pay the same for things today as he did twenty years ago.

at a loss
unable to make a response or find a solution
When a man stopped me in the street and said I was his long-lost brother, I was quite at a loss.

as a rule
generally
As a rule I go to bed before eleven.

in any case
even if other factors are disregarded
We can't refund your money on a watch which was broken through your own carelessness. In any case, the guarantee has already expired.

Ask and answer

1. (times) Why couldn't the company keep up with its competitors?
2. (balance) Who will win the election?
3. (loss) How did you feel when the boss called you an incompetent fool?
4. (whole) What did you think of the last film you saw?
5. (record) Why were the Minister's remarks not published?

Complete the sentence

1. (run) The killer escaped from prison and now ...
2. (rule) I sometimes get up early on Sundays, but ...
3. (point) Whether or not you want to come is ...
4. (case) I don't want to play tennis. It's too cold and ...
5. (way) It's a nice party, isn't it? My name's ...

On your own

Make up sentences using these ten idioms.

SECTION 8.3

Complete the sentence

(in the long run, in the first place, at short notice, for good measure, in due course)

1. They never loved each other, so I don't know why they got married...
2. It's difficult to find a babysitter...
3. The car salesman gave me a car radio...
4. Elegant clothes cost a lot of money, but they are worth it...
5. Mike will know if he's been accepted at university...

In your own words

1. I accepted this ten-pound note without realising that it was a forgery. (faith)
2. 'The last bus has just gone.'
   'Then we'll have to take a taxi.' (case)
3. My house was certainly not cheap. (means)
4. I've just failed my law exams again. If this continues, I'll never be a lawyer. (rate)
5. We are talking about different subjects. (purposes)

On your own

Make up sentences using these ten idioms.

in the long run   opposite **in the short run**
> over a long period
> *We hope to make a profit in the long run.*

in due course
> at some foreseeable time or date, according to the ordinary sequence of events
> *You will be informed of the results of your examination in due course.*

in the first place
> initially
> *I don't care if the party is cancelled, because I didn't want to go in the first place.*

in good faith
> with honest intentions
> *I bought that car in good faith, not realising that it was stolen.*

in that case
> if that is so
> A. *That British Airways flight is completely full.*
> B. *Really? In that case, I'll go by Air France.*

at this rate
> if the present rate of progress continues
> *I thought it would take a month to decorate the house, but at this rate it'll take a year.*

at short notice
> with little advance warning
> *You can't expect me to cook dinner for ten people at such short notice.*

at cross-purposes
> misunderstanding (each other)
> *I'm afraid we're speaking at cross-purposes. Let me explain myself once more.*

by no means
> certainly not
> *I've by no means forgiven him for his rude behaviour.*

for good measure
> in addition to the agreed amount
> *She paid me what we agreed, plus five pounds for good measure.*

SECTION 8.4

1. **out of date**

   These machines are out of date. We must buy some new ones.

2. **out of order**

   The petrol pumps were out of order, so I had to go to another petrol station.

3. **out of hand**

   When the demonstration got out of hand and a riot started, the organisers called the police.

4. **out of touch (with someone)**

   John and I have been out of touch since he went to work in Australia.

5. **out of bounds (to someone)**

   This is a military airfield and it is out of bounds to civilians.

6. **out of favour (with someone)**

   Peter criticised his boss yesterday and now he's out of favour.

7. **out of the question**

   When I asked a friend if I could borrow her car, she said it was out of the question.

8. **out of the running**

   He lost in the second round of the tournament, so he's out of the running now.

9. **out of (one's) mind**

   He plans to cross the Sahara on roller skates. He must be out of his mind.

10. **out of (one's) hands**

    I have reported the incident to the police and now the matter is out of my hands.

Work it out

Try to work out the meanings of the idioms on this page from the example sentences and then write in the definitions. Check your answers in the key at the back of the book or in a dictionary.

On your own

Make up sentences using these ten idioms.

PREPOSITION-NOUN-
PREPOSITION COMBINATIONS

In Sections 9.1, 9.2 and 9.3, nouns are used idiomatically and meanings given as usual. The nouns in Section 9.4, however, are used literally and so definitions are not given.

■ A few expressions change in the following way. *For the sake of (someone/something)* can take the alternative form *for (someone's/ something's) sake.*

■ All idioms in this unit are followed by a noun or gerund, except *in order to* which is followed by a verb.

■ Some idioms may look very similar, but have in fact completely different meanings

in case of (something)	if (something) happens
in the case of	in the instance of

■ Most of the expressions presented in this unit are invariable
He's making a profit at the expense of his friends.

SECTION 9.1

in spite of
> despite
> *He continued to smoke in spite of his doctor's advice.*

on behalf of   also **on (someone's) behalf**
> as a representative of
> *On behalf of the company, I should like to wish Mr Smith a happy retirement.*

on account of
> because of
> *The train was late on account of a signal failure.*

by means of
> using
> *He unlocked the car door by means of a hairpin.*

by virtue of
> being authorised or justified by
> *By virtue of my authority as the captain of this ship, I order the arrest and confinement of that man.*

in view of
> considering ☆
> *The judge decided not to send the thief to prison in view of the fact that he was 94 years old.*

in common with
> like
> *Henrik has blonde hair and blue eyes, in common with most Scandinavians.*

in league with   also **in collusion with**
> allied to (usually secretly)
> *Were the Japanese in league with the Germans when they attacked Pearl Harbour in 1941?*

in accordance with
> following (plans, instructions)
> *In accordance with our orders, we attacked the enemy from behind.*

in touch with
> communicating/able to communicate with
> *I haven't seen Peter for several years, but I'm still in touch with him.*

Complete the sentence

1. (account) The yacht race was cancelled...
2. (spite) My grandfather is very healthy...
3. (behalf) I filled out the application form...
4. (league) The soldier was arrested when his superiors found out that...
5. (touch) I haven't met George recently, but I am still...

Join the sentences

1. (common) Tigers eat meat. Many animals eat meat.
2. (means) I opened the can. I used a screwdriver.
3. (accordance) He posted the letter. He obeyed his father's instructions.
4. (view) Henry was promoted. He has worked for this company for a long time.
5. (virtue) I claim this treasure. I am the person who found it.

On your own

Make up sentences using these ten idioms. Use a dictionary to find the other meanings of idioms marked ☆.

SECTION 9.2

Complete the sentence

(in return for, with respect to, in the name of, on the strength of, on the part of)

1. My foreign friends were very kind to me, so ... their kindness, I invited them to my home.
2. Cortez and Pizarro destroyed South American civilisation ... Christianity.
3. The strike was due to stubbornness ... the management.
4. The teacher made several comments ... the student's attitude.
5. He tried to get away with not studying hard ... his popularity among the teachers.

Ask and answer

1. (order) Why are you studying English?
2. (form) How would you express thanks to a friend?
3. (face) Why was the soldier given a medal?
4. (odds) Why did the referee speak to the goalkeeper?
5. (course) When is it most likely to snow?

On your own

Make up sentences using these ten idioms.

in order to
   with the purpose of
   I go to work by bicycle in order to save money.

in return for
   as compensation for
   In return for your kindness, I'd like to give you this small present.

with respect to   also **with regard to**
   concerning
   Your suggestion is helpful with respect to our present situation.

at odds with
   in disagreement with (someone over something)
   They are always at odds with each other over how to bring up their children.

in the course of
   during
   In the course of my lifetime I have met many strange people.

in the name of
   purporting to serve
   Many ancient cultures have been destroyed in the name of progress.

in the face of
   despite (danger)
   The early Christians preached in Rome in the face of terrible persecution.

in the form of   also **in the shape of**
   appearing as
   My colleagues conveyed their gratitude in the form of a digital wrist-watch.

on the part of   also **on (someone's) part**
   done or felt by
   Mistakes have been made on the part of both the government and the civil service.

on the strength of
   relying on
   I was able to borrow a lot of money on the strength of my father's reputation at the bank.

SECTION 9.3

in case of
if something happens
*In case of fire, break the glass case and press the
alarm button.*

in charge of
supervising or controlling
*This is Captain Brace, who's in charge of this
ship and its crew.*

in consideration of
because of
*We invited him to our wedding in consideration
of his having introduced us to each other.*

in danger of
likely to (with bad consequences)
*When the tanker caught fire, its cargo of crude
oil was in danger of exploding.*

(be) in favour of
support
*Five directors were in favour of the proposal
and three were against it.*

(be) in honour of
commemorate, show respect for
*Every year, on 2 March, the company has a
special holiday in honour of its founder.*

(be) in need of
require
*Because of the drought last summer, we're in
need of water.*

in place of   also **in (someone's) place**
instead of
*The dealer gave me a new watch in place of the
defective one I had returned to him.*

in possession of
possessing
*The police are now in possession of documents
which show that the minister accepted bribes.*

in time of
where there is/was (need, want, trouble)
*I am grateful to him because he helped me in
time of need.*

Complete the sentence

1. (danger) Two hundred employees . . .
   losing their jobs because of the
   recession.
2. (charge) Who . . . this operation?
3. (need) Doctors in Bangladesh . . .
   medicine.
4. (possession) He was arrested for . . .
   drugs.
5. (favour) Most schoolchildren . . .
   abolishing uniforms.

In your own words

1. (place) The council built a new hospital
   to replace the one which was destroyed
   by the earthquake.
2. (honour) I propose a toast to show my
   respect for the President.
3. (time) My friends always comfort me
   when I'm in trouble.
4. (case) The army will support the
   government if there's a revolution.
5. (consideration) He was promoted
   because of his outstanding ability.

On your own

Make up sentences using these ten idioms.

SECTION 9.4

Ask and answer

1. (basis) How did the jury decide whether the accused was innocent or guilty?
2. (sake) Why did John take up running?
3. (advice) Why did she buy new spectacles?
4. (hope) Why are you studying English?
5. (sight) When did the soldiers begin to desert?

Join the sentences

1. (exchange) She bought him a drink. He gave her a free ticket to the concert.
2. (exception) I've read all his books but one. I haven't read 'The Third Man'.
3. (habit) Susan loves the cinema. She goes every week.
4. (expense) Their parents went to the Bahamas for a month last year. They couldn't afford to buy their children any new clothes.
5. (addition) She gets a newspaper every morning. She also buys several magazines each week.

On your own

Make up sentences using these ten idioms.

in the habit of
> *I'm in the habit of drinking a glass of whisky every evening before going to bed.*

in the hope of
> *I went to the cinema early in the hope of getting a good seat.*

on the basis of
> *They decided to cut defence spending on the basis of several ministry reports.*

at the expense of also **at (someone's) expense**
> *The shareholders are making huge profits at the expense of the workers, who are underpaid.*

at the sight of
> *She fainted at the sight of her dead husband.*

for the sake of also **for (someone's) sake**
> *He gave up his political career for the sake of his family.*

with the exception of
> *I have visited every country in Europe, with the exception of Finland.*

on the advice of also **on (someone's) advice**
> *I gave up smoking on the advice of my doctor.*

in exchange for
> *The tourist gave the old man her watch in exchange for his painting.*

in addition to
> *In addition to my salary, I get a time-keeping bonus.*

PREPOSITION-ADVERB AND
PREPOSITION-ADJECTIVE COMBINATIONS

The important point about these idioms is not the grammatical function of the individual words that make up each idiom, but the grammatical function of the complete idiom.

■ The idioms in Sections 10.1 and 10.2 are used adverbially and those in Section 10.3 as prepositions. The ten idioms in Section 10.4 are used as adverbs, adjectives, prepositions or modifiers.

SECTION 10.1

In your own words

1. (first) When I first met him, I thought he was very unfriendly.
2. (ever) I wish I could stay here until I die.
3. (usual) Mr Smith caught the 8.23 express train, as he does most mornings.
4. (yet) I've been wanting to write a novel for years, but until now I haven't had any good ideas.
5. (well) During my holiday I'm going to go wind-surfing and I'm also going to go water-skiing.

Complete the sentence

1. (least) During this course, I hope to learn...
2. (once) There has been a serious accident. Please call...
3. (last) I failed the exam many times, but I persevered and...
4. (once) I thought the snake was asleep, but...
5. (once) My girlfriend is almost always late, but yesterday evening...

On your own

Make up sentences using these ten idioms.

at once
immediately
If you don't leave at once, I shall call the police.

at first
initially
I tried to reason with her at first, but then I gave up.

at last
finally
We seemed to be climbing forever, but at last we reached the summit.

at least
if not more
Even if you didn't like the present, you should at least have said 'thank you'.

as usual
as usually happens
John arrived late for work, as usual.

as yet
until now
He graduated last month, but as yet he hasn't found a job.

as well   also **as well as (someone/something)**
in addition
He has a big house in London, and a villa in Spain as well.

for once
on this occasion unlike previous occasions
The boss accepted my request, for once.

for ever   also **for good**
permanently
I plan to live in England for ever.

all at once
suddenly
I was walking through the park at lunchtime, when all at once the sky went black.

SECTION 10.2

all along
since the beginning
I pretended to be surprised at his death, but in fact I had known all along that he was seriously ill.

all told
in total
All told, there were sixty people on board.

above all
most important
A successful salesman must be friendly, dynamic and, above all, persuasive.

after all
despite what was said or expected ☆
Her parents disapproved of the marriage, but they went to the wedding after all.

all in all
as an overall assessment
All in all, the party was a success.

for now also **for the time being**
at present and for a short time
We can manage with the old photocopier for now, but please send the new one as soon as possible.

as of now
at this time
As of now, the police haven't discovered the identity of the killer.

from now on
starting now and continuing in the foreseeable future
From now on, all drivers are legally required to wear seat belts.

just now
a moment ago ☆
I saw an ambulance outside your house just now. Is anything wrong?

so far
until now
I bought this car last year and so far I've had no trouble with it.

Complete the sentence

(Use an idiom containing **all**.)

1. We had a few bad experiences, but . . . our trip was very pleasant.
2. An artist needs skill, patience and, . . . , imagination.
3. Including the crew, . . . 216 people died in the plane crash.
4. The police didn't arrest the dealer until he contacted his customers, although they knew . . . that he was carrying heroin.
5. Everyone expected the party to be cancelled, but it was held . . .

Complete the sentence

(Use an idiom containing **now** or **far**.)

1. He was involved in a traffic accident . . . , and he's still shocked.
2. I haven't studied hard so far, but . . . I'm going to make more effort.
3. Rescuers are exploring the wreckage of the plane, but . . . they haven't found any survivors.
4. My new job will not start until next year, so I shall continue to work for my present employer . . .
5. I'm looking for a picture for the sitting room, but . . . I haven't found one.

On your own

Make up sentences using these ten idioms. Use a dictionary to find the other meanings of idioms marked ☆.

SECTION 10.3

Complete the sentence

1. (regardless of) The fireman ran into the burning hotel, . . .
2. (according to) America was discovered by Columbus, . . .
3. (owing to) . . ., many workers lost their jobs.
4. (but for) The fire would have destroyed the building, . . .
5. (such as) I like modern composers, . . .

In your own words

1. (for all) He enjoys his job, although he's always complaining.
2. (subject to) My plan to go round the world depends on whether or not I can get the necessary visas.
3. (contrary to) I expected to fail the exam, but I passed it.
4. (as for) The strikers will forfeit their wages. Their leaders will lose their jobs.
5. (as to) Can you give me some advice about choosing a career?

On your own

Make up sentences using these ten idioms.

but for   also **if it were not for**
> if (something) had not been available
> *I would have drowned, but for my lifebelt.*

as for
> concerning
> *The art gallery is to be demolished. As for its collection of paintings, they will be sold by auction.*

as to
> concerning
> *The advertisement said nothing as to the type of work involved.*

owing to
> because of
> *Owing to the bad weather, the match was cancelled.*

according to
> as stated by
> *The world will end in 1999, according to Nostradamus.*

contrary to
> opposite to, different from
> *Contrary to our expectations, the party was very interesting.*

subject to
> conditional upon
> *Our plans to build a supermarket here are subject to the approval of the town council.*

regardless of
> notwithstanding
> *I am determined to interview the guerrilla leader, regardless of the danger involved.*

such as
> for example
> *I like Impressionist painters, such as Dégas and Van Gogh, very much.*

for all
> despite
> *For all her mistakes, she's done a very good job.*

SECTION 10.4

1. **all right**

   I was ill last week, but I'm all right now.

2. **at all**

   I had some money yesterday, but now I haven't got any at all.

3. **in general**

   I don't like big cities in general, but I think Paris is very beautiful.

4. **in short**

   He's rude, bad-tempered and conceited – in short, he's a very unpleasant man.

5. **in full**

   You must write your name and address in full on any job application form.

6. **as far as**

   As far as I know, there are no sharks in Lake Geneva.

7. **as long as**

   You may borrow my car, as long as you promise to drive carefully.

8. **so as to**

   A fence was built along the canal, so as to prevent anyone from falling in.

9. **by far**

   Mount Fuji is by far the highest mountain in Japan.

10. **and so on**

    My job is to design public buildings, such as museums, libraries, stations and so on.

Work it out

Try to work out the meanings of the idioms on this page from the example sentences and then write in the definitions. Check your answers in the key at the back of the book or in a dictionary.

On your own

Make up sentences using these ten idioms.

11 ADJECTIVE-NOUN COMBINATIONS

In Sections 11.1 and 11.2 of this unit, adjectives are used idiomatically and nouns are used literally
> *tall story*
> *practical joke*

■ In Section 11.3, adjectives and nouns are used idiomatically, and Section 11.4 includes both types.

■ The combinations behave as nouns. In most cases only the noun takes a plural form
> *tall story*　*tall stories*

SECTION 11.1

cold war
    unfriendly relations between nations, but with
      no military engagement
    The Cold War between NATO and the Warsaw
      Pact countries reached its peak in the sixties.

tall story
    an exaggerated and unbelievable tale
    He tells so many tall stories that no one believes
      anything he says.

blind date
    an arranged meeting between two people who
      have never met before
    Mike and Janet met on a blind date and have
      hated each other ever since.

sweeping statement
    a wide generalisation
    I disagreed with his sweeping statement about
      middle-class values.

open secret
    supposedly-secret fact known to many people
    It's an open secret that the headmistress is
      about to resign.

practical joke
    a trick played on a person
    His practical jokes are usually quite funny, but
      putting salt in my tea wasn't funny.

universal rule
    a rule applicable to all cases
    Many people say that red wine with meat and
      white wine with fish is a universal rule.

golden opportunity
    an excellent and rare opportunity
    This heat wave is a golden opportunity for the
      makers of air conditioners and fans.

rough guess   also **rough estimate**
    an approximate estimate
    At a rough guess, I should say this company has
      600 employees.

package tour
    a tour in which transport, accommodation and
      itinerary are pre-arranged by a travel
      company
    This package tour of Europe looks interesting.

Complete the sentence

1. (date) I met her on ... arranged by a
   friend.
2. (secret) He hasn't told anyone about his
   illness, but ...
3. (war) Many contemporary spy novels
   are set during ...
4. (joke) When they told me there was a
   bomb in my suitcase, I didn't realise ...
5. (tour) Do you prefer to travel
   independently or ... ?

Find the idiom

1. All English people drink tea.
2. Water is safe to drink if you boil and
   filter it first.
3. I had always wanted to start my own
   business, and then two years ago I won
   £5,000 in a lottery.
4. I saw an elephant playing a violin last
   time I went to the circus.
5. There are about four thousand million
   people on our planet.

On your own

Make up sentences using these ten idioms.

SECTION 11.2

Ask and answer

1. (punishment) What's the purpose of the electric chair in the USA?
2. (sense) How did you know that the plane was going to crash?
3. (office) What do companies do when they want to develop new markets?
4. (conclusion) Why weren't people surprised when the champion won the tournament again?
5. (battery) What's wrong with your car?

Complete the sentence

1. (smokers) Many busy executives . . .
2. (hate) I dislike salespeople. In fact, they're . . .
3. (benefits) My salary isn't very high, but . . .
4. (order) We are supplied with typing paper every week. The firm has . . .
5. (store) Our local grocer's was sold to a large company and now . . .

On your own

Make up sentences using these ten idioms.

branch office
> a subsidiary office
> *We are planning to open a branch office in Paris soon.*

flat battery
> a battery which no longer generates electricity
> *I left my car headlights on all night and had a flat battery in the morning.*

fringe benefit
> a benefit given as a supplement to wages
> *In addition to your salary, we offer fringe benefits including luncheon vouchers, health insurance and parking facilities.*

foregone conclusion
> an inevitable or predictable result
> *The re-election of the government was a foregone conclusion.*

pet hate   also **pet aversion**
> someone/something one particularly dislikes
> *Spiders are my pet hate.*

chain store
> one in a group of stores owned by the same person or company
> *A new chain store has just opened in my neighbourhood.*

chain smoker
> a person who smokes cigarettes continuously
> *My boss is a chain smoker.*

standing order
> instruction to a dealer or bank to supply something regularly over a fixed period
> *I have a standing order with my local dairy for two pints of milk a day.*

capital punishment
> the death penalty
> *Capital punishment was abolished many years ago.*

sixth sense
> intuition
> *I couldn't see in the dark, but my sixth sense warned me that I was being followed.*

SECTION 11.3

weak point   opposite **strong point**
   a weak or defective area
   Grammar is my weak point.

sore point
   a subject which upsets or annoys
   *Dogs have been a sore point with him ever since
   he was bitten by one.*

vicious circle
   an unbroken, circular sequence of cause and
   effect, with bad results
   *Inflation is a vicious circle. Higher prices lead to
   higher wages which lead to higher prices.*

going concern
   a viable business
   *My parents started their business with very
   little money, but now it's definitely a going
   concern.*

tight corner
   a difficult or dangerous situation
   *His knowledge of karate often got him out of a
   tight corner.*

square deal   also **fair deal**
   a fair agreement
   *My old car plus £500 for your new car? I think
   that's a fair deal.*

cross-section
   a representative selection
   *We interviewed a cross-section of the
   community to find out their feelings about the
   proposed new motorway.*

happy medium
   a satisfactory compromise between extremes
   *I dislike summer and winter and I find spring is a
   happy medium.*

soap opera
   a sentimental domestic drama
   *Television soap operas are very popular these
   days.*

saving grace
   a quality which compensates for deficiencies
   His cheerfulness is his only saving grace.

Complete the sentence

1. He worked as a spy for ten years and
   was often in ...
2. I'll probably fail my maths exam
   because maths is ...
3. The company lost a lot of money at
   first, but now it ...
4. There's so much drama in our family
   history, it's like ...
5. The manager was planning to change
   the company's pension system, so he
   decided to discuss it with ...

Find the idiom

1. I would rather you didn't talk about my
   relationship with Mary.
2. Whenever I drive my friend to work in
   my car, he pays for the petrol.
3. Although he's lazy and often borrows
   money without repaying it, he's very
   kind to people.
4. My illness is due to overwork, but if I
   don't work hard I can't earn enough
   money to pay my medical bills.
5. My friend wanted to live in the city, but
   I preferred the country, so we bought a
   house in the suburbs.

On your own

Think of a situation to illustrate each of
these ten idioms.

SECTION 11.4

Work it out

Try to work out the meanings of the idioms on this page from the example sentences and then write in the definitions. Check your answers in the key at the back of the book or in a dictionary.

On your own

Make up sentences using these ten idioms.

1. **white lie**

   When I said I thought her novel was good, it was a white lie.

2. **green belt**

   Construction of offices and factories is not allowed in the green belt around London.

3. **black market**

   When the American Government banned the sale of alcohol in the twenties, a black market selling alcohol at high prices was soon established.

4. **green light**

   I've been trying to get my idea accepted for years, and finally I got the green light last week.

5. **red tape**

   There was so much red tape involved in trying to claim a tax rebate, that I gave up in the end.

6. **rush hour**

   Trains are always crowded during the rush hour and almost empty the rest of the day.

7. **short cut**

   I know a short cut to the station which takes ten minutes less than the usual route.

8. **final fling**

   The old man decided to have a final fling and spent all his savings on a world tour.

9. **old hand**

   She never makes mistakes because she's been here so long and is an old hand at the job.

10. **wishful thinking**

    I know it may be wishful thinking, but I believe the publishers will accept my novel.

12 NOUN PHRASES

Each idiom in this unit is made up of two nouns, where one or both of the two nouns may be used idiomatically
> *sandwich course* ('course' is used literally)
> *rat race* (both nouns are used idiomatically)

■ Many of these idioms come from metaphors
> *gunboat diplomacy* (from the era when gunboats were sent to
>   enforce political demands)

■ Most of these idioms are variable. When a noun phrase is used in the plural, only the second noun becomes plural
> *family trees*
> *status symbols*

SECTION 12.1

Complete the sentence

1. From the top of the Eiffel Tower you get...
2. She bought an expensive car as...
3. During the flu epidemic our office was run by...
4. Hoping to get a job in chemical research, I took...
5. You can see who my ancestors were by looking at...

Find the idiom

1. Everyone is struggling to get a better position in society.
2. The young and the old don't understand each other.
3. The powerful country threatened to start a war against its small neighbours if they refused to cooperate.
4. The population of the country doubled in ten years.
5. People frequently offer encouragement to others without really caring.

On your own

Make up sentences using these ten idioms.

sandwich course
a course of study which alternates theoretical and practical training
I'm doing a sandwich course in electronic engineering at the local college.

skeleton staff
the minimum number of personnel with which an office or factory can manage
The office is run by a skeleton staff at Christmas.

bird's-eye view
a view from above
You get a bird's-eye view of the town from the castle.

gunboat diplomacy
diplomacy backed by fierce or military threats
Many small countries were forced by the gunboat diplomacy of bigger nations to give up territories.

population explosion
a rapid increase in population
The population explosion in England in the eighteenth century was partly the result of falling infant mortality rates.

family tree
a chart showing someone's ancestry
My family tree shows that we originally came from France, but married into an English family 200 years ago.

rat race
competitive struggle in work or society
He dropped out of the rat race and retired to the country.

generation gap
the difference between the attitudes of young and old people
The generation gap often causes teenagers to run away from home.

lip-service
insincere expression of support
He said it was a good plan, but I think it was only lip-service.

status symbol
a material object intended to indicate one's wealth or importance
Joe's had a swimming pool built in the back garden as a status symbol now that he's rich.

SECTION 12.2

balance of mind
sanity
He killed his parents while his balance of mind was disturbed.

presence of mind
ability to think calmly in a crisis
Thanks to the pilot's presence of mind, the burning plane landed safely.

cash on delivery
cash payment made for goods when they are delivered
You can pay cash on delivery at our special discount rate, or if you prefer we'll invoice you by post at the normal rate.

blessing in disguise
something which appears bad at first but turns out well
Missing the train was a blessing in disguise because it crashed.

slip of the tongue
a careless, spoken error
I didn't mean to say that. It was a slip of the tongue.

slip of the pen
a careless, written error
Be careful when you write out contracts. A slip of the pen might cost you a lot of money.

man/woman of letters
a scholar
This university has produced many great men of letters.

man/woman of his/her word
someone who fulfils his or her promises
You can rely on Chris. He's a man of his word.

man/woman of the world
someone with wide experience
My aunt was a woman of the world.

the man/woman in the street
the average citizen
What does the man in the street think about the plan to increase taxes?

Complete the sentence

1. She always keeps her promises. She is ...
2. I carelessly wrote £1,000 on the cheque, instead of £100. It was ...
3. I failed to get the job I had applied for, but the company went bankrupt soon after. It was ...
4. You must pay for the goods at the time of delivery. We only accept payment ...
5. I didn't want to let out your secret. It was ...

In your own words

1. When a fire started in a night club, the waiter led the guests calmly to the fire escape.
2. They confined him when he became insane.
3. Plato wrote several great works.
4. I always ask my boss for advice about anything, because she's had a lot of experience.
5. Wise politicians pay attention to the opinions of the average person.

On your own

Make up sentences using these ten idioms.

SECTION 12.3

Complete the sentence

1. (eye) A fish jumped out of the water and then vanished again ...
2. (mouth) Before the age of newspapers, news usually circulated ...
3. (time) We arrived at the station ...
4. (moment) I saw a parrot in a pet shop window and decided to buy it ...
5. (heart) I wish to thank you for looking after me ...

Ask and answer

1. (tongue) Have you remembered that name yet? No, but ...
2. (teeth) Did you pass your exam? Yes, ...
3. (thinking) English is an easy language, isn't it? No, ...
4. (fact) Would you like to buy this car? No, I ...
5. (course) Did you have to bribe the customs official to approve your application for an export licence? No, ...

On your own

Make up sentences using these ten idioms.

as a matter of fact
actually
No, I'm not a bachelor. As a matter of fact, I've been married for twenty years.

as a matter of course
in accordance with normal procedure
It isn't necessary to ask for a rise. Your salary will be increased each year as a matter of course.

on the spur of the moment
impulsively
I packed my bag and left for Europe on the spur of the moment.

on the tip of (one's) tongue
not quite able to remember something
I'll remember her name in a moment. It's on the tip of my tongue.

in the twinkling of an eye
in an instant
The pickpocket took my wallet and disappeared in the twinkling of an eye.

in the nick of time
just in time
A car came round the corner at high speed and I stepped back onto the pavement in the nick of time.

by the skin of (one's) teeth
scarcely avoiding (failure, disaster)
I just caught the plane by the skin of my teeth.

by word of mouth
orally
We heard about the company's bankruptcy by word of mouth. The directors haven't written to us about it yet.

from the bottom of (one's) heart
sincerely
I wish you success from the bottom of my heart.

to (one's) way of thinking
in my opinion
To my way of thinking, cars should be kept out of central London.

13 IDIOMS FROM METAPHORS

There are many idioms derived from metaphors, ranging from single words

bottleneck
thunderstruck

to entire sentences

A lot of water has passed under the bridge.

■ It is sometimes possible to guess the origins of these idioms. *Rock the boat* and *plain sailing* obviously have nautical origins. *On the cards* and *lay one's cards on the table* come from gambling expressions. Others are rather less obvious. *Bury the hatchet* comes from American Indian peace-making ceremonies.

■ Section 13.1 presents adjective-noun combinations, Section 13.2 preposition-noun combinations, Section 13.3 noun phrases and Section 13.4 presents verbal expressions.

SECTION 13.1

Find the idiom

1. I was walking along when a tile fell from a roof above and smashed at my feet.
2. His family haven't spoken to him since he married a foreigner despite their objections.
3. Knowing that the man he was after liked horse-racing, the detective went to the racecourse to look for him.
4. We have climbed the hardest part of the mountain. From now on, it will be easy.
5. Developing our product on those lines was a disaster. There was no market.

Complete the sentence

1. After weeks of paying endless bills, his cut in salary was . . .
2. We never use this microwave oven you bought us. It's turned out to be . . .
3. His comment about sausages when we were discussing the world food problem was . . .
4. He's always criticising your luxury flat, but in my opinion it's just . . .
5. The Berlin Wall is a concrete symbol of . . .

On your own

Make up sentences using these ten idioms.

white elephant
a useless possession
Our house is full of white elephants, such as this ashtray shaped like a bottle of ink.

red herring
an irrelevant or misleading diversion
We were discussing exams, when Mike introduced a red herring by asking our opinions on corporal punishment in schools.

black sheep
someone who doesn't obey his/her family or group conventions
My family treat me as the black sheep because I'm a hot dog seller and not a doctor like my father and two brothers.

close shave
narrow escape from danger or misfortune
I had a close shave today. I stepped into the road and was nearly killed by a bus.

long shot
an enterprise with little chance of success
It's a long shot, but we should ask the police if anyone has handed in a wallet.

blind alley
an enterprise with no future
You're in a blind alley looking for a job here.

sour grapes
pretending one dislikes something one secretly wants but can't have
He says cars pollute the atmosphere and should be banned, but it's just sour grapes because he can't afford to buy one.

plain sailing
a trouble-free situation or course of action
I have passed the most difficult test. From now on, it's plain sailing all the way.

Iron Curtain
an ideological barrier between capitalist and socialist countries of Europe
Life behind the Iron Curtain is supposed to be very different from life in the West.

last straw
the ultimate provocation
When the waiter brought me cold soup, it was the last straw and I complained to the manager.

SECTION 13.2

in a rut
    in a way of life with no prospect of change
    When I realised I was in a rut, I left the village
    where I lived and moved to London.

in the dark   also **keep (someone) in the dark**
    uninformed
    Sorry to have kept you in the dark about my
    new job, but I didn't want to tell anyone until
    it was certain.

in the running   opposite **out of the running**
    competing with a chance of winning
    Most of our swimmers failed to qualify for the
    Olympic Games, but four of them are still in
    the running.

in the limelight
    the focus of public attention
    Elvis Presley was in the limelight almost all his life.

on the cards
    quite likely
    It's on the cards that the minister will resign
    because of the scandal.

in the red   opposite **in the black**
    in debt
    Our company has been operating in the red for
    several years.

on tenterhooks
    tense while awaiting the outcome of something
    I've been on tenterhooks ever since I heard that
    I was being considered for the job.

on the rocks
    about to fail
    His marriage is on the rocks and his wife has
    applied for a divorce.

off the cuff
    without preparation
    I had no time to prepare a speech, so I said a few
    words off the cuff.

behind the scenes
    behind the public facade
    The management and union have been
    negotiating behind the scenes to prevent a
    strike.

Complete the sentence

1. Film stars are accustomed to being...
2. The peace treaty was concluded thanks to a lot of discussion...
3. A general election is...
4. Due to the slump in exports, the balance of trade is...
5. I won my game in the fourth round of the chess tournament, so...

Ask and answer

1. Why were the shareholders so angry about the directors' decision to merge with another company?
2. Why is the company president so worried?
3. How are you supposed to feel when you read suspense novels?
4. Why did the speaker hesitate so often?
5. Why did you leave your last job?

On your own

Make up sentences using these ten idioms.

SECTION 13.3

Find the idiom

1. A politician was treated to dinner by a rich industrialist. The press immediately accused him of accepting a bribe.
2. He asked me to guess how much he'd sold his house for, so I said £100,000, but I couldn't really judge.
3. Their offer to accept fifty refugees is totally inadequate.
4. The reduction in interest rates will help small companies which are struggling to survive.
5. My colleague told the boss that I was trying to form a union.

Complete the sentence

1. (wolf) Until my cousin claimed a share of my grandfather's inheritance, I didn't realise...
2. (flash) His first record sold over 100,000 copies, but...
3. (iceberg) That riot last week in the local prison was just...
4. (bolt) My uncle wrote to me and offered me a job in America. It was...
5. (ointment) The rail strike on the day of the wedding was...

On your own

Make up ten sentences using these idioms.

tip of the iceberg
> a minor problem indicating the existence of a much greater problem
> *Isolated incidents of vandalism are just the tip of the iceberg.*

shot in the dark   similar to **long shot**
> a haphazard guess
> *I couldn't quite remember the man's name, but I tried a shot in the dark and called him Mr Black.*

drop in the ocean
> a contribution that is almost worthless because such a huge amount is needed
> *Any money I give to charity is merely a drop in the ocean.*

flash in the pan
> a success that only lasts a short time
> *People expected him to become world champion, but it seems his initial success was just a flash in the pan.*

shot in the arm
> a stimulus
> *The new export orders will be a shot in the arm for the shipbuilding industry.*

storm in a teacup
> an exaggerated incident
> *The alleged scandal was just a storm in a teacup.*

fly in the ointment
> a minor incident that interferes with one's enjoyment of something.
> *It was a very pleasant evening, although Janet being sick on the carpet was a fly in the ointment.*

bolt from the blue
> an unexpected and very surprising event
> *The letter from the old man's solicitor saying that I had inherited his entire fortune was a bolt from the blue.*

snake in the grass
> a treacherous person
> *Don't trust George with your secrets. He's a snake in the grass.*

wolf in sheep's clothing
> an enemy pretending to be a friend
> *She seemed quite charming, but she turned out to be a wolf in sheep's clothing.*

SECTION 13.4

1. **break the ice**

   The party started quietly, so I introduced a few people to each other so as to break the ice.

2. **bury the hatchet**

   The two families had been feuding for years, but finally they buried the hatchet.

3. **rock the boat**

   We have a nice profitable company. Don't rock the boat by trying to change our methods.

4. **miss the boat**

   I applied for the job as soon as I saw the advertisement, but I missed the boat.

5. **ring a bell**

   William Smith? The name rings a bell. Wasn't he one of the speakers at the last conference?

6. **smell a rat**

   When I saw the salesman wink at his partner, I smelled a rat.

7. **take root**

   The Women's Liberation movement received little support at first, but now it's beginning to take root.

8. **bear fruit**

   Our advertising campaign is starting to bear fruit. Sales have risen this month.

9. **split hairs**

   All right, I admit that cigars are different from cigarettes, but let's not split hairs. They are both bad for the health.

10. **pull strings**

    George knows some local politicians and he pulled a few strings to get his son a job.

Work it out

Try to work out the meanings of the idioms on this page from the example sentences and then write in the definitions. Check your answers in the key at the back of the book or in a dictionary.

On your own

Make up sentences using these ten idioms.

14 VERBAL IDIOMS FROM METAPHORS

The idioms presented in this unit are all verbal idioms which have their origins in metaphors.

SECTION 14.1

call the tune
  have control over what other people do
  The assistant manager said, 'While the manager is on holiday, I am calling the tune!'

weather the storm
  survive a period of difficulty
  My wife is in hospital and I've just lost my job. I hope I can weather the storm.

give the game away
  reveal someone's plans
  My friends were planning a surprise birthday party for me but one of them gave the game away.

sit on the fence
  remain uncommitted or neutral
  The chairman is reluctant to comment on this issue and prefers to sit on the fence.

get off the track
  be diverted from the main subject of conversation
  I think we are getting off the track. We were talking about television programmes, not films.

beat about the bush
  avoid speaking directly about something
  Please stop beating about the bush and say exactly what you mean.

play for time
  cause a delay in order to gain time
  When the robber entered the bank, the clerk sounded the police alarm and then played for time.

come to light
  become known
  New evidence came to light which proved the man was wrongly arrested.

hold water
  be viable
  If we test your theory, I think we'll find that it doesn't hold water.

carry weight
  be influential
  The assistant manager's opinions carry a lot of weight in this office.

Complete the sentence

1. (bush) He never says what he means. He always...
2. (tune) While I am in charge of this theatre, I...
3. (light) Just recently, several public housing scandals...
4. (track) Forgive me for interrupting you, but I think...
5. (storm) When the rate of interest went up, people stopped buying new houses and many builders...

Ask and answer

1. (weight) Do newspapers influence public opinion?
2. (water) Why did you reject my theory?
3. (fence) Has he decided which argument to support?
4. (game) How did the police find out that he was a smuggler?
5. (time) What would you do if you were held up at gunpoint?

On your own

Make up sentences using these ten idioms.

SECTION 14.2

Complete the sentence

1. (trumpet) He thinks highly of himself and is always . . .
2. (fingers) You should be careful when speculating in land, otherwise . . .
3. (hand) We can't plan our strategy for dealing with the opponents of our project until they . . .
4. (foot) When I asked her how her boyfriend was, I . . .
5. (toes) During the first month, new employees . . .

Ask and answer

1. (nest) How did the treasurer of the charity fund manage to buy such a big house?
2. (guns) What do you do when people contradict you and you're sure that you're right?
3. (weight) Why is the new foreman unpopular?
4. (foot) What did Mr Harris do when his daughter kept on arriving home after midnight?
5. (oats) Why didn't Paul get a job and settle down as soon as he graduated from university?

On your own

Make up sentences using these ten idioms.

show (one's) hand also **lay (one's) cards on the table**
reveal (one's) true intentions
The bilateral treaty talks have made no progress yet because each side is reluctant to show its hand.

burn (one's) fingers
suffer injury or loss after a risky venture
He invested a lot of money in the stock market without professional advice and burned his fingers.

put (one's) foot down
insist on something
I'm going to put my foot down. From now on you will not watch television at all until you have finished your homework.

put (one's) foot in it
make an embarrassing mistake
I really put my foot in it when I congratulated her on her new job in front of the boss.

blow (one's) own trumpet
boast
Forgive me for blowing my own trumpet, but I do think I'm quite a good artist.

feather (one's) nest
profit secretly
While the company was losing money, the Managing Director was feathering his nest.

keep on (one's) toes also **stay on (one's) toes**
stay alert
The teacher kept asking questions at random to keep her pupils on their toes.

stick to (one's) guns
insist on one's point of view
We all told him he was wrong, but he stuck to his guns.

sow (one's) wild oats
enjoy a life of pleasure while young
He's only twenty two. Let him sow his wild oats, and he'll soon settle down.

throw (one's) weight about/around
exercise authority in an oppressive way
That actress is always throwing her weight around during rehearsals and upsetting the rest of the cast.

SECTION 14.3

take (someone) for a ride
deceive someone
That salesman took me for a ride when he persuaded me what a good car this was.

pull (someone's) leg
tease someone
When he told me he'd won £25,000, I thought he was pulling my leg.

put a spoke in (someone's) wheel
hinder or prevent something
He wanted to build an ugly factory, but I put a spoke in his wheel by refusing to sell my land.

follow in (someone's) footsteps
do as someone else did before
My friend's daughter has decided to follow in her father's footsteps and become a politician.

step into (someone's) shoes
succeed someone
When the boss retires, I hope to step into his shoes.

take a leaf out of (someone's) book
follow someone's example
I took a leaf out of my friend's book when I exchanged my fast car for an economic one.

turn the tables on (someone)
reverse the position in one's favour
My opponent won the first two games, but then I managed to turn the tables on him.

meet (someone) halfway
compromise
The employee asked for a twelve per cent rise. The manager offered him eight per cent. They eventually met halfway and agreed to ten per cent.

play second fiddle to (someone)
take second place
I won't play second fiddle to Dr Barnes on this expedition.

catch (someone) red-handed
catch someone in the act of committing a crime
They caught the thief red-handed as he tried to escape with the stolen goods in his bag.

Find the idiom

1. My friend told me that a tiger had escaped from the zoo and was in my neighbourhood, but it wasn't true.
2. I became an engineer, just as my father did twenty-five years ago.
3. When I bought this ring, the salesman told me it was made of gold. A week later I discovered that it was only brass.
4. The builder said it would take three months to build the house, but the customer wanted to move in within two months. The builder agreed to finish the house in ten weeks.
5. He was walking out of the shop with the calculator in his pocket, when the store detective put a hand on his shoulder.

Complete the sentence

1. (spoke) He intended to convert the old hotel into a pub, but opposition from the neighbours ...
2. (fiddle) The boss will retire soon. Until then, I am willing ...
3. (leaf) My brother went to Canada and got a good job. I am planning ...
4. (tables) My sister refused to lend me her car, so I bought my own. Last week her car broke down and now I intend to ...
5. (shoes) When the company president retires, his son will probably ...

On your own

Make up sentences using these ten idioms.

SECTION 14.4

Work it out

Try to work out the meanings of the idioms on this page from the example sentences and then write in the definitions. Check your answers in the key at the back of the book or in a dictionary.

On your own

Make up sentences using these idioms.

1. **hit the nail on the head**

   When she said that the company was too old-fashioned, she hit the nail on the head.

2. **let the cat out of the bag**   also **spill the beans**

   By telling the press about our plans for a new model, you've let the cat out of the bag.

3. **burn the candle at both ends**

   My doctor said, 'If you continue to work so hard all day and study all evening you'll be ill. You're burning the candle at both ends.'

4. **make a mountain out of a mole-hill**

   I complained strongly when I found my colleague reading my newspaper but he told me not to make a mountain out of a mole-hill.

5. **jump out of the frying pan into the fire**

   I changed my job because it was boring, but I soon realised I had jumped out of the frying pan into the fire.

6. **have a skeleton in the cupboard/closet**

   Mr and Mrs Peters seemed a perfect couple, but they had a skeleton in the cupboard. During the war, they had spied for the enemy.

7. **take the bull by the horns**

   When something goes wrong, you should take the bull by the horns and face up to it.

8. **flog a dead horse**

   People who keep trying to persuade him to change his mind are flogging a dead horse.

9. **turn over a new leaf**

   He used to be a thief, but then he turned over a new leaf and now has his own shop.

10. **get hold of the wrong end of the stick**

    I'm afraid you've got hold of the wrong end of the stick. That lady is my wife, not this one.

15 SHORT IDIOMS

Many nouns with idiomatic origins are used as ordinary nouns. *Pickpocket*, for example, comes from the expression *pick (someone's) pocket*.

■ Often these nouns are derived from phrasal verbs. *Breakdown*, for example, comes from the verb *break down*. Here are some more examples

bypass	**outlay**	**runaway**
intake	**outlet**	**setback**
layout	**outset**	**upbringing**
outburst	**pickup**	**upkeep**
outcast		
outflow		

■ Some are hyphenated

fall-out	**mix-up**	**stand-by**
hold-up	**out-cry**	**take-off**
lay-by	**sell-out**	**turn-out**
look-out	**set-up**	
make-up	**show-off**	

■ Sections 15.1 and 15.2 present two-word adjectives derived from idioms, and Section 15.3 presents common verbs with idiomatic functions. Section 15.4 presents common prepositions which function idiomatically and which can only be used after the verb *to be*.

SECTION 15.1

In your own words

1. She was extremely unhappy when her husband died.
2. He's never bought me a drink in all the years I've known him.
3. The corners of this book are damaged, so we can't sell it at full price.
4. He made twenty people redundant without feeling at all sorry for them.
5. Don't waste time arguing with him. He never changes his mind.

Complete the sentence

1. (absent-minded) She was supposed to be coming to dinner yesterday, but she forgot. She...
2. (tight-lipped) Several people tried to get information about next season's fashion designs, but the designers...
3. (big-headed) He used to be modest and quiet, but now...
4. (high-handed) My new supervisor...
5. (light-fingered) Recent research has shown that severe depression causes people...

On your own

Make up sentences using these ten idioms.

dog-eared
with damaged corners (papers, books)
I've been using my dog-eared, old set of encyclopaedias for years now.

pig-headed
obstinate
He's pig-headed and never listens to the advice of others.

tight-fisted
mean (with money)
He's so tight-fisted that he reads other people's newspapers instead of buying his own.

absent-minded
forgetful
Our absent-minded teacher forgot to bring our books yesterday and forgot the chalk today.

tight-lipped
uncommunicative
The architect was very tight-lipped about the plans for the shopping precinct, but described the housing estate in detail.

big-headed
vain
I don't know why he's so big-headed. He's got nothing to boast about.

broken-hearted
very sad
He was broken-hearted when his son died. He had no one else in the world.

high-handed
overbearing
The new manager is high-handed and so his staff dislike him.

cold-blooded
callous
He's a cold-blooded murderer, completely unmoved by the suffering of his victims and their families.

light-fingered
one who often steals
Store detectives are looking out for light-fingered customers.

SECTION 15.2

second-hand
  something having a previous owner
  *I often buy second-hand clothes, if they're in
    reasonable condition.*

easy-going
  tolerant and relaxed
  *My flat-mate is very easy-going and we never
    quarrel.*

long-winded
  talk at great or unnecessary length
  *Everyone fell asleep during his long-winded
    speech about butterflies.*

tongue-tied
  too shy or embarrassed to speak freely
  *Whenever a teacher speaks to me, I get
    tongue-tied.*

off-beat
  unconventional
  *There's an interesting, off-beat jazz club near
    my house.*

word-perfect
  perfectly-memorised
  His recitation of the poem was word-perfect.

all-round
  versatile (used only before nouns)
  *He's a good all-round sportsman. He's good at
    football, tennis, golf and badminton.*

off-peak   similar to **off-season**
  when consumption (gas, electricity) or
    congestion (traffic) is below maximum
  *Train tickets are cheaper if you travel during
    off-peak periods.*

well-to-do   also **well off**
  wealthy
  *My brother married a well-to-do
    businesswoman.*

brand-new
  absolutely new
  *I always buy brand-new shoes, rather than
    second-hand ones.*

Ask and answer

1. When is it cheapest to travel by plane?
2. Do you always play a particular
   position on the soccer field? No, ...
3. Do actors have to learn their lines
   thoroughly? Yes, ...
4. Do you ever buy second-hand clothes?
   No, ...
5. Does she often quarrel with people?
   No, ...

Complete the sentence

1. I didn't have enough money to buy a
   new stereo, so I bought ...
2. I couldn't understand his explanation
   because ...
3. She used to stammer as a child and she
   still ...
4. People in the street always stop and
   stare at him because he wears ...
5. His family used to be poor and working
   class, but now ...

On your own

Make up sentences using these ten idioms.

SECTION 19.3

Ask and answer

1. (names) Why did the boy hit his sister?
2. (lurch) What did your guide do when your bus broke down in the desert?
3. (turn) Why are you grateful to your friend?
4. (ring) What would you do if you wanted to speak to someone in a hurry?
5. (granted) Why might Europeans waste paper?

Complete the sentence

1. (surprise) My sudden promotion...
2. (hiding) I told the child that if he picked flowers from my garden again...
3. (picture) My brother told me there'd been a family row, so I rang my mother and she...
4. (hand) I couldn't carry the heavy table by myself so I asked my brother...
5. (line) As soon as you find out what time your plane arrives in London, please...

On your own

Make up sentences using these ten idioms.

give (someone) a ring
telephone someone
Please give me a ring some time next week.

give (someone) a hiding
beat someone severely
Every time she came home late, her father gave her a hiding.

drop (someone) a line
send a letter to someone
As soon as I reach Australia, I'll drop you a line.

lend (someone) a hand   also **give (someone) a hand**
help someone
Would you mind lending me a hand to carry this box, please?

call (someone) names
insult someone
The new foreman is unpopular because he calls everyone names.

do (someone) a good/bad turn
do something which benefits/harms someone
He helped me to find a job and I later thanked him for doing me a good turn.

take (someone) by surprise
surprise someone
The Prime Minister's death took the nation by surprise.

take (something) for granted
assume (the availability/truth) of
I took water for granted until I went for a trip through the desert.

leave (someone) in the lurch
abandon someone when he/she needs help
When our money and passports were stolen, our travel agent left us in the lurch.

put (someone) in the picture   also **keep (someone) in the picture**
inform someone or keep someone informed
The director, who had been away for a week, didn't know about the new contract, so we put her in the picture.

SECTION 19.4

break the news to (someone)
inform someone of good/bad news
The policeman broke the news of his father's death to him.

have a word with (someone)
speak to someone (often confidentially)
May I have a word with you about your son?

steal a march on (someone)
gain advantage by doing something earlier than expected
National Electric was planning to market their new computer next year, but we stole a march on them by putting a similar model on the market last month.

take (one's) cue from (someone)
follow someone's example
I had never used chopsticks before, but I took my cue from my Chinese hosts.

break (someone's) heart
make someone deeply sad
She broke my heart when she rejected my proposal of marriage.

get on (someone's) nerves
irritate someone
Don't keep walking up and down. It gets on my nerves.

take (someone's) word for (something)
believe someone
I wasn't informed that the party had been cancelled, but I'll take your word for it.

take (someone's) mind off (something)
help someone stop thinking about something
We made her enter the tennis tournament to take her mind off her impending exam.

take (someone's) point
accept someone's argument
We must get the Arts Centre finished this year, but I take your point that the housing project is more urgent.

call (someone's) bluff
challenge someone to do what they've threatened to do
The hijacker threatened to kill the pilot. The pilot eventually called his bluff and walked slowly to the door of the aeroplane.

Complete the sentence

1. (nerves) I wish you would stop whistling because...
2. (news) We decided to get married and the next day we telephoned her parents to...
3. (mind) She was worried about starting her new job, so I took her to see a film to...
4. (word) My train really was late. Why don't you telephone the station if you won't...
5. (cue) I didn't know what to do at the wedding so I watched the other guests and ...

In your own words

1. (point) He convinced me that his argument was correct.
2. (word) I spoke to your father about this matter.
3. (bluff) The salesman claimed the watch was unbreakable, so the customer dropped it to prove he was lying.
4. (march) 'The Times' reported the incident a day before the other newspapers.
5. (heart) She made her mother very sad when she went to live in Canada.

On your own

Make up sentences using these ten idioms.

SECTION 19.3

Ask and answer

1. (names) Why did the boy hit his sister?
2. (lurch) What did your guide do when your bus broke down in the desert?
3. (turn) Why are you grateful to your friend?
4. (ring) What would you do if you wanted to speak to someone in a hurry?
5. (granted) Why might Europeans waste paper?

Complete the sentence

1. (surprise) My sudden promotion . . .
2. (hiding) I told the child that if he picked flowers from my garden again . . .
3. (picture) My brother told me there'd been a family row, so I rang my mother and she . . .
4. (hand) I couldn't carry the heavy table by myself so I asked my brother . . .
5. (line) As soon as you find out what time your plane arrives in London, please . . .

On your own

Make up sentences using these ten idioms.

give (someone) a ring
telephone someone
Please give me a ring some time next week.

give (someone) a hiding
beat someone severely
Every time she came home late, her father gave her a hiding.

drop (someone) a line
send a letter to someone
As soon as I reach Australia, I'll drop you a line.

lend (someone) a hand   also **give (someone) a hand**
help someone
Would you mind lending me a hand to carry this box, please?

call (someone) names
insult someone
The new foreman is unpopular because he calls everyone names.

do (someone) a good/bad turn
do something which benefits/harms someone
He helped me to find a job and I later thanked him for doing me a good turn.

take (someone) by surprise
surprise someone
The Prime Minister's death took the nation by surprise.

take (something) for granted
assume (the availability/truth) of
I took water for granted until I went for a trip through the desert.

leave (someone) in the lurch
abandon someone when he/she needs help
When our money and passports were stolen, our travel agent left us in the lurch.

put (someone) in the picture   also **keep (someone) in the picture**
inform someone or keep someone informed
The director, who had been away for a week, didn't know about the new contract, so we put her in the picture.

SECTION 19.4

break the news to (someone)
  inform someone of good/bad news
  The policeman broke the news of his father's death to him.

have a word with (someone)
  speak to someone (often confidentially)
  May I have a word with you about your son?

steal a march on (someone)
  gain advantage by doing something earlier than expected
  National Electric was planning to market their new computer next year, but we stole a march on them by putting a similar model on the market last month.

take (one's) cue from (someone)
  follow someone's example
  I had never used chopsticks before, but I took my cue from my Chinese hosts.

break (someone's) heart
  make someone deeply sad
  She broke my heart when she rejected my proposal of marriage.

get on (someone's) nerves
  irritate someone
  Don't keep walking up and down. It gets on my nerves.

take (someone's) word for (something)
  believe someone
  I wasn't informed that the party had been cancelled, but I'll take your word for it.

take (someone's) mind off (something)
  help someone stop thinking about something
  We made her enter the tennis tournament to take her mind off her impending exam.

take (someone's) point
  accept someone's argument
  We must get the Arts Centre finished this year, but I take your point that the housing project is more urgent.

call (someone's) bluff
  challenge someone to do what they've threatened to do
  The hijacker threatened to kill the pilot. The pilot eventually called his bluff and walked slowly to the door of the aeroplane.

Complete the sentence

1. (nerves) I wish you would stop whistling because...
2. (news) We decided to get married and the next day we telephoned her parents to...
3. (mind) She was worried about starting her new job, so I took her to see a film to...
4. (word) My train really was late. Why don't you telephone the station if you won't...
5. (cue) I didn't know what to do at the wedding so I watched the other guests and ...

In your own words

1. (point) He convinced me that his argument was correct.
2. (word) I spoke to your father about this matter.
3. (bluff) The salesman claimed the watch was unbreakable, so the customer dropped it to prove he was lying.
4. (march) 'The Times' reported the incident a day before the other newspapers.
5. (heart) She made her mother very sad when she went to live in Canada.

On your own

Make up sentences using these ten idioms.

20 EVERYDAY EXPRESSIONS

Many idiomatic expressions are used in daily conversation. These are often polite phrases used in specific situations as a matter of custom.

greeting
> *How are you?   How have you been?   How are you getting on?*
> *How's things?*

being introduced
> *How do you do?   Pleased to meet you.*

responding to thanks
> *Not at all.   Don't mention it.   That's all right.   You're welcome.*

giving/refusing permission
> *Certainly.   By all means.*
> *I'm afraid...   I'm sorry, but...*

making, accepting and refusing invitations
> *Would you like to...?   Would you care to...?*
> *How about...?   Do you want to...?*
> *Yes, I'd love to...   Yes, please.*
> *Thanks all the same, but...   No, thanks.*

responding to apologies
> *That's quite all right.   Don't mention it.*

congratulating
> *Well done!   Congratulations!*

sympathising
> *I'm very sorry to hear that.*

offering condolence
> *Never mind.*

encouraging
> *Good luck!   Best of luck!   All the best!*

SECTION 20.1

on second thoughts
changing a previous statement
I'll have a beer. No, on second thoughts I'll have orange juice. I have to drive home.

on the other hand
from the opposite point of view
Package holidays are very convenient. On the other hand, they don't give you much freedom.

for that matter
indeed, moreover
I would certainly object if an airport were built near here. So, for that matter, would most of the local people.

for one thing
as one reason
I hate my job. For one thing, the hours are too long. For another, the wages are low.

all things considered
considering all relevant factors
All things considered, I think you were very lucky to have escaped injury when the plane crashed.

by all accounts
from what one has heard
By all accounts, it was the worst storm we've ever had in this area.

to tell you the truth
to speak frankly
Some friends have asked me to their party this evening, but to tell you the truth, I'd rather not go.

all the same
nevertheless
I know the other driver was going too fast, but all the same, by not stopping, you were partly to blame for the accident.

not to mention   also **let alone**
even if we don't consider
Increases in tax will be opposed by big business, not to mention small firms.

what's more
furthermore
I haven't got a television and what's more, I don't want one.

Complete the sentence

1. Spain is a good place to spend a holiday. For one thing...
2. Thatched roofs look nicer than tiled ones, but on the other hand...
3. I'd like two small loaves of bread. On second thoughts...
4. My job is very interesting. What's more...
5. The critics said that film was rubbish. All the same...

In your own words

1. (matter) I don't like the new manager. Neither, indeed, does anyone else.
2. (truth) I went to see the Picasso exhibition, but actually I didn't enjoy it.
3. (considered) Considering the cost, the itinerary and the service, I was very satisfied with my holiday.
4. (accounts) Everyone seemed to think it was an excellent play.
5. (mention) I'm looking forward to sunbathing, and of course swimming.

On your own

Make up sentences using these ten idioms.

20 EVERYDAY EXPRESSIONS

Many idiomatic expressions are used in daily conversation. These are often polite phrases used in specific situations as a matter of custom.

greeting
How are you? How have you been? How are you getting on? How's things?

being introduced
How do you do? Pleased to meet you.

responding to thanks
Not at all. Don't mention it. That's all right. You're welcome.

giving/refusing permission
Certainly. By all means.
I'm afraid... I'm sorry, but...

making, accepting and refusing invitations
Would you like to...? Would you care to...?
How about...? Do you want to...?
Yes, I'd love to... Yes, please.
Thanks all the same, but... No, thanks.

responding to apologies
That's quite all right. Don't mention it.

congratulating
Well done! Congratulations!

sympathising
I'm very sorry to hear that.

offering condolence
Never mind.

encouraging
Good luck! Best of luck! All the best!

SECTION 20.1

on second thoughts
changing a previous statement
I'll have a beer. No, on second thoughts I'll have orange juice. I have to drive home.

on the other hand
from the opposite point of view
Package holidays are very convenient. On the other hand, they don't give you much freedom.

for that matter
indeed, moreover
I would certainly object if an airport were built near here. So, for that matter, would most of the local people.

for one thing
as one reason
I hate my job. For one thing, the hours are too long. For another, the wages are low.

all things considered
considering all relevant factors
All things considered, I think you were very lucky to have escaped injury when the plane crashed.

by all accounts
from what one has heard
By all accounts, it was the worst storm we've ever had in this area.

to tell you the truth
to speak frankly
Some friends have asked me to their party this evening, but to tell you the truth, I'd rather not go.

all the same
nevertheless
I know the other driver was going too fast, but all the same, by not stopping, you were partly to blame for the accident.

not to mention also **let alone**
even if we don't consider
Increases in tax will be opposed by big business, not to mention small firms.

what's more
furthermore
I haven't got a television and what's more, I don't want one.

Complete the sentence

1. Spain is a good place to spend a holiday. For one thing . . .
2. Thatched roofs look nicer than tiled ones, but on the other hand . . .
3. I'd like two small loaves of bread. On second thoughts . . .
4. My job is very interesting. What's more . . .
5. The critics said that film was rubbish. All the same . . .

In your own words

1. (matter) I don't like the new manager. Neither, indeed, does anyone else.
2. (truth) I went to see the Picasso exhibition, but actually I didn't enjoy it.
3. (considered) Considering the cost, the itinerary and the service, I was very satisfied with my holiday.
4. (accounts) Everyone seemed to think it was an excellent play.
5. (mention) I'm looking forward to sunbathing, and of course swimming.

On your own

Make up sentences using these ten idioms.

Find the idiom

1. After teasing the dog like that, he deserved to be bitten and I'm glad he was.
2. He isn't at all concerned whether he finds a job or not.
3. She thinks I deliberately misled her, but she's completely mistaken.
4. You don't have to go if you don't want to.
5. The fact that his brother is a Member of Parliament is irrelevant.

Ask and answer

1. (difference) Shall we have lunch in a pub or in a restaurant?
2. (business) How are you going to break the news to him?
3. (what) I had to sew a button on my jacket last night.
4. (helped) Were you sorry when you had to come home from holiday a week early? Yes, but . . .
5. (things) Aren't you upset about your purse being stolen? No, not really, . . .

On your own

Make up sentences using these ten idioms.

SECTION 20.2

mind (one's) own business
not interfere or pry
He asked me how much I earned and I told him to mind his own business.

please (one)self
do as you like
'Would you like a cigarette?' 'No, thanks. Smoking is bad for the health.' 'Please yourself.'

(that's) neither here nor there
that's irrelevant, unimportant
'Can I borrow your car?' 'But you've never driven a Mini.' 'That's neither here nor there.'

couldn't care less
not care at all
I couldn't care less if I never see you again.

so what?   also **what of it?**
what significance does that have? (implying no significance)
'Your mother disapproves of your behaviour.' 'So what? I'm not a child and I do as I please.'

nothing could be further from the truth
that's completely wrong
'But surely you were dismissed?' 'Nothing could be further from the truth. I left because I didn't like the way they operated.'

(it) serves (someone) right
someone deserves to suffer a bad result
'I was late for the play and they wouldn't let me in.' 'It serves you right. You're always late.'

(it) can't be helped
it can't be avoided or prevented
The concert has been cancelled because of the snow. It's a pity, but it can't be helped.

(it's) just one of those things
such things inevitably happen occasionally
We missed our plane because of the rail strike. It was just one of those things.

(it) makes no difference
it doesn't matter
It makes no difference whether the party is on Friday or Monday because I'm free both days.

SECTION 20.3

(it) stands to reason (that)
 it's logical to conclude that
 It stands to reason that people work harder if
 they enjoy their jobs.

(it) goes without saying (that)
 it's obvious that
 It goes without saying that if you retire early,
 you won't be entitled to a pension.

(it's) no wonder (that)
 it isn't surprising that
 It's no wonder that he has trouble with his liver.
 He drinks five pints of beer a day.

(it's) a good job (that)
 it's fortunate that
 It's a good job that the bus wasn't carrying any
 passengers when it crashed.

(it) just so happens (that)
 in fact, although you may not realise this
 'Look! We're running out of petrol. I told you
 we should have bought some at the last
 garage.'
 'It just so happens that I have a spare can of
 petrol.'

(it's) just as well
 it's fortunate in the circumstances
 It's raining. It's just as well I remembered to
 bring my umbrella.

(it's) high time   also **(it's) about time**
 something must be done immediately (and
  should have already been done)
 It's high time the council built a pedestrian
 crossing here. There have already been
 several accidents.

(it's) no secret (that)
 it's a well-known fact that
 It's no secret that this company has been losing
 money for several years.

rumour has it (that)
 it's rumoured that
 Rumour has it that a general election will be
 called this summer.

(I) take it (that)
 I assume that
 'What an awful noise!'
 'I take it you don't like my new record.'

In your own words

1. (rumour) Lots of people seem to think the cricket tour will be cancelled.
2. (take) She assumed I was unhappy because I wasn't smiling.
3. (high time) We really must take those books back to the library immediately.
4. (wonder) I wasn't surprised when the river flooded after all that rain.
5. (job) It's lucky that I cooked plenty of food. I didn't know you were bringing friends home.

Complete the sentence

1. It ... that we'll celebrate your birthday, but what would you like to do?
2. It ... that you'll be tired after such a long walk.
3. It ... that you're getting married next month, you know.
4. It ... that I did pay the bill. I have the receipt in my pocket.
5. It ... that I decided not to work for that firm. They have just gone bankrupt.

On your own

Make up sentences using these ten idioms.

Find the idiom

1. After teasing the dog like that, he deserved to be bitten and I'm glad he was.
2. He isn't at all concerned whether he finds a job or not.
3. She thinks I deliberately misled her, but she's completely mistaken.
4. You don't have to go if you don't want to.
5. The fact that his brother is a Member of Parliament is irrelevant.

Ask and answer

1. (difference) Shall we have lunch in a pub or in a restaurant?
2. (business) How are you going to break the news to him?
3. (what) I had to sew a button on my jacket last night.
4. (helped) Were you sorry when you had to come home from holiday a week early? Yes, but . . .
5. (things) Aren't you upset about your purse being stolen? No, not really, . . .

On your own

Make up sentences using these ten idioms.

SECTION 20.2

mind (one's) own business
> not interfere or pry
> *He asked me how much I earned and I told him to mind his own business.*

please (one)self
> do as you like
> *'Would you like a cigarette?' 'No, thanks. Smoking is bad for the health.' 'Please yourself.'*

(that's) neither here nor there
> that's irrelevant, unimportant
> *'Can I borrow your car?' 'But you've never driven a Mini.' 'That's neither here nor there.'*

couldn't care less
> not care at all
> *I couldn't care less if I never see you again.*

so what?   also **what of it?**
> what significance does that have? (implying no significance)
> *'Your mother disapproves of your behaviour.' 'So what? I'm not a child and I do as I please.'*

nothing could be further from the truth
> that's completely wrong
> *'But surely you were dismissed?'*
> *'Nothing could be further from the truth. I left because I didn't like the way they operated.'*

(it) serves (someone) right
> someone deserves to suffer a bad result
> *'I was late for the play and they wouldn't let me in.' 'It serves you right. You're always late.'*

(it) can't be helped
> it can't be avoided or prevented
> *The concert has been cancelled because of the snow. It's a pity, but it can't be helped.*

(it's) just one of those things
> such things inevitably happen occasionally
> *We missed our plane because of the rail strike. It was just one of those things.*

(it) makes no difference
> it doesn't matter
> *It makes no difference whether the party is on Friday or Monday because I'm free both days.*

SECTION 20.3

(it) stands to reason (that)
  it's logical to conclude that
  *It stands to reason that people work harder if
  they enjoy their jobs.*

(it) goes without saying (that)
  it's obvious that
  *It goes without saying that if you retire early,
  you won't be entitled to a pension.*

(it's) no wonder (that)
  it isn't surprising that
  *It's no wonder that he has trouble with his liver.
  He drinks five pints of beer a day.*

(it's) a good job (that)
  it's fortunate that
  *It's a good job that the bus wasn't carrying any
  passengers when it crashed.*

(it) just so happens (that)
  in fact, although you may not realise this
  *'Look! We're running out of petrol. I told you
  we should have bought some at the last
  garage.'*
  *'It just so happens that I have a spare can of
  petrol.'*

(it's) just as well
  it's fortunate in the circumstances
  *It's raining. It's just as well I remembered to
  bring my umbrella.*

(it's) high time also **(it's) about time**
  something must be done immediately (and
  should have already been done)
  *It's high time the council built a pedestrian
  crossing here. There have already been
  several accidents.*

(it's) no secret (that)
  it's a well-known fact that
  *It's no secret that this company has been losing
  money for several years.*

rumour has it (that)
  it's rumoured that
  *Rumour has it that a general election will be
  called this summer.*

(I) take it (that)
  I assume that
  'What an awful noise!'
  'I take it you don't like my new record.'

In your own words

1. (rumour) Lots of people seem to think
   the cricket tour will be cancelled.
2. (take) She assumed I was unhappy
   because I wasn't smiling.
3. (high time) We really must take those
   books back to the library immediately.
4. (wonder) I wasn't surprised when the
   river flooded after all that rain.
5. (job) It's lucky that I cooked plenty of
   food. I didn't know you were bringing
   friends home.

Complete the sentence

1. It ... that we'll celebrate your birthday,
   but what would you like to do?
2. It ... that you'll be tired after such a
   long walk.
3. It ... that you're getting married next
   month, you know.
4. It ... that I did pay the bill. I have the
   receipt in my pocket.
5. It ... that I decided not to work for that
   firm. They have just gone bankrupt.

On your own

Make up sentences using these ten idioms.

SECTION 20.4

Work it out

Try to work out the meanings of the idioms on this page from the example sentences and then write in the definitions. Check your answers in the key at the back of the book or in a dictionary.

On your own

Make up sentences using these ten idioms.

1. **can't stand**

   I can't stand having to be polite to people whom I dislike.

2. **can't help**

   I can't help smoking even though I know it's bad for my health.

3. **can't imagine**

   I can't imagine why you want to come into the office at weekends as well!

4. **wouldn't dream of**

   'Let me pay you for your help.'
   'I wouldn't dream of accepting payment from a friend.'

5. **(it's) no use** also **there's no use in**

   It's no use studying English if you never have a chance to use it.

6. **(it's) (well) worth**

   The cinema will be crowded, so it's worth making a seat reservation in advance.

7. **there's no harm in**

   I expect he'll refuse your request, but there's no harm in asking.

8. **there's no point in** also **see no point in**

   There's no point in going to the pub with us if you don't like drinking.

9. **(it) wouldn't do (for someone) to**

   It wouldn't do for the mayor to arrive late for the ceremony.

10. **(it) pays/doesn't pay to**

    It pays to have your car serviced regularly.

KEY

Unit 1, p. 9

1. explode
2. rise into the air
3. try to impress people
4. become cheerful, recover from depression
5. become calm
6. put on one's best clothes
7. expand the range of one's business
8. happen unexpectedly
9. faint
10. recover consciousness

Unit 2, p. 14

1. record spoken words in writing
2. delete
3. put clothes on to see if they fit
4. draft (a document, plan)
5. complete appropriate spaces (in a document, form)
6. distribute
7. withdraw (a statement, criticism)
8. mention (a subject)
9. make comfortable by using/wearing
10. purchase all available stocks

Unit 3, p. 19

1. do repeatedly
2. continue
3. continue
4. suddenly start
5. want to
6. choose, like
7. receive, inherit
8. want very much
9. reach the end of
10. consider something a bad thing

Unit 4, p. 24

1. leave
2. attend
3. become uncontrollable
4. try to notice
5. not go near
6. interrupt
7. do or get belatedly (news, sleep)
8. feel superior to
9. become involved or obsessed with
10. do (mischief)

Unit 5, p. 29

1. be forgotten
2. change one's idea or intention
3. decide
4. speak frankly
5. become insane
6. work as hard as one's fellows
7. withdraw one's remarks
8. be sufficient
9. achieve distinction
10. think hard

Unit 6, p. 34

1. assume control of
2. be offended by
3. look after
4. pity
5. acknowledge one's merit in doing
6. consider
7. be proud of
8. avenge oneself on
9. look enquiringly at
10. grasp

SECTION 20.4

Work it out

Try to work out the meanings of the idioms on this page from the example sentences and then write in the definitions. Check your answers in the key at the back of the book or in a dictionary.

On your own

Make up sentences using these ten idioms.

1. **can't stand**

   I can't stand having to be polite to people whom I dislike.

2. **can't help**

   I can't help smoking even though I know it's bad for my health.

3. **can't imagine**

   I can't imagine why you want to come into the office at weekends as well!

4. **wouldn't dream of**

   'Let me pay you for your help.'
   'I wouldn't dream of accepting payment from a friend.'

5. **(it's) no use**   also **there's no use in**

   It's no use studying English if you never have a chance to use it.

6. **(it's) (well) worth**

   The cinema will be crowded, so it's worth making a seat reservation in advance.

7. **there's no harm in**

   I expect he'll refuse your request, but there's no harm in asking.

8. **there's no point in**   also **see no point in**

   There's no point in going to the pub with us if you don't like drinking.

9. **(it) wouldn't do (for someone) to**

   It wouldn't do for the mayor to arrive late for the ceremony.

10. **(it) pays/doesn't pay to**

    It pays to have your car serviced regularly.

KEY

Unit 1, p. 9

1. explode
2. rise into the air
3. try to impress people
4. become cheerful, recover from depression
5. become calm
6. put on one's best clothes
7. expand the range of one's business
8. happen unexpectedly
9. faint
10. recover consciousness

Unit 2, p. 14

1. record spoken words in writing
2. delete
3. put clothes on to see if they fit
4. draft (a document, plan)
5. complete appropriate spaces (in a document, form)
6. distribute
7. withdraw (a statement, criticism)
8. mention (a subject)
9. make comfortable by using/wearing
10. purchase all available stocks

Unit 3, p. 19

1. do repeatedly
2. continue
3. continue
4. suddenly start
5. want to
6. choose, like
7. receive, inherit
8. want very much
9. reach the end of
10. consider something a bad thing

Unit 4, p. 24

1. leave
2. attend
3. become uncontrollable
4. try to notice
5. not go near
6. interrupt
7. do or get belatedly (news, sleep)
8. feel superior to
9. become involved or obsessed with
10. do (mischief)

Unit 5, p. 29

1. be forgotten
2. change one's idea or intention
3. decide
4. speak frankly
5. become insane
6. work as hard as one's fellows
7. withdraw one's remarks
8. be sufficient
9. achieve distinction
10. think hard

Unit 6, p. 34

1. assume control of
2. be offended by
3. look after
4. pity
5. acknowledge one's merit in doing
6. consider
7. be proud of
8. avenge oneself on
9. look enquiringly at
10. grasp

SECTION 19.3

Ask and answer

1. (names) Why did the boy hit his sister?
2. (lurch) What did your guide do when your bus broke down in the desert?
3. (turn) Why are you grateful to your friend?
4. (ring) What would you do if you wanted to speak to someone in a hurry?
5. (granted) Why might Europeans waste paper?

Complete the sentence

1. (surprise) My sudden promotion . . .
2. (hiding) I told the child that if he picked flowers from my garden again . . .
3. (picture) My brother told me there'd been a family row, so I rang my mother and she . . .
4. (hand) I couldn't carry the heavy table by myself so I asked my brother . . .
5. (line) As soon as you find out what time your plane arrives in London, please . . .

On your own

Make up sentences using these ten idioms.

give (someone) a ring
telephone someone
Please give me a ring some time next week.

give (someone) a hiding
beat someone severely
Every time she came home late, her father gave her a hiding.

drop (someone) a line
send a letter to someone
As soon as I reach Australia, I'll drop you a line.

lend (someone) a hand also **give (someone) a hand**
help someone
Would you mind lending me a hand to carry this box, please?

call (someone) names
insult someone
The new foreman is unpopular because he calls everyone names.

do (someone) a good/bad turn
do something which benefits/harms someone
He helped me to find a job and I later thanked him for doing me a good turn.

take (someone) by surprise
surprise someone
The Prime Minister's death took the nation by surprise.

take (something) for granted
assume (the availability/truth) of
I took water for granted until I went for a trip through the desert.

leave (someone) in the lurch
abandon someone when he/she needs help
When our money and passports were stolen, our travel agent left us in the lurch.

put (someone) in the picture also **keep (someone) in the picture**
inform someone or keep someone informed
The director, who had been away for a week, didn't know about the new contract, so we put her in the picture.

SECTION 19.4

break the news to (someone)
inform someone of good/bad news
The policeman broke the news of his father's death to him.

have a word with (someone)
speak to someone (often confidentially)
May I have a word with you about your son?

steal a march on (someone)
gain advantage by doing something earlier than expected
National Electric was planning to market their new computer next year, but we stole a march on them by putting a similar model on the market last month.

take (one's) cue from (someone)
follow someone's example
I had never used chopsticks before, but I took my cue from my Chinese hosts.

break (someone's) heart
make someone deeply sad
She broke my heart when she rejected my proposal of marriage.

get on (someone's) nerves
irritate someone
Don't keep walking up and down. It gets on my nerves.

take (someone's) word for (something)
believe someone
I wasn't informed that the party had been cancelled, but I'll take your word for it.

take (someone's) mind off (something)
help someone stop thinking about something
We made her enter the tennis tournament to take her mind off her impending exam.

take (someone's) point
accept someone's argument
We must get the Arts Centre finished this year, but I take your point that the housing project is more urgent.

call (someone's) bluff
challenge someone to do what they've threatened to do
The hijacker threatened to kill the pilot. The pilot eventually called his bluff and walked slowly to the door of the aeroplane.

Complete the sentence

1. (nerves) I wish you would stop whistling because . . .
2. (news) We decided to get married and the next day we telephoned her parents to . . .
3. (mind) She was worried about starting her new job, so I took her to see a film to . . .
4. (word) My train really was late. Why don't you telephone the station if you won't . . .
5. (cue) I didn't know what to do at the wedding so I watched the other guests and . . .

In your own words

1. (point) He convinced me that his argument was correct.
2. (word) I spoke to your father about this matter.
3. (bluff) The salesman claimed the watch was unbreakable, so the customer dropped it to prove he was lying.
4. (march) 'The Times' reported the incident a day before the other newspapers.
5. (heart) She made her mother very sad when she went to live in Canada.

On your own

Make up sentences using these ten idioms.

20 EVERYDAY EXPRESSIONS

Many idiomatic expressions are used in daily conversation. These are often polite phrases used in specific situations as a matter of custom.

greeting
> *How are you?   How have you been?   How are you getting on?*
> *How's things?*

being introduced
> *How do you do?   Pleased to meet you.*

responding to thanks
> *Not at all.   Don't mention it.   That's all right.   You're welcome.*

giving/refusing permission
> *Certainly.   By all means.*
> *I'm afraid...   I'm sorry, but...*

making, accepting and refusing invitations
> *Would you like to...?   Would you care to...?*
> *How about...?   Do you want to...?*
> *Yes, I'd love to...   Yes, please.*
> *Thanks all the same, but...   No, thanks.*

responding to apologies
> *That's quite all right.   Don't mention it.*

congratulating
> *Well done!   Congratulations!*

sympathising
> *I'm very sorry to hear that.*

offering condolence
> *Never mind.*

encouraging
> *Good luck!   Best of luck!   All the best!*

SECTION 20.1

on second thoughts
    changing a previous statement
    I'll have a beer. No, on second thoughts I'll have
    orange juice. I have to drive home.

on the other hand
    from the opposite point of view
    Package holidays are very convenient. On the
    other hand, they don't give you much
    freedom.

for that matter
    indeed, moreover
    I would certainly object if an airport were built
    near here. So, for that matter, would most of
    the local people.

for one thing
    as one reason
    I hate my job. For one thing, the hours are too
    long. For another, the wages are low.

all things considered
    considering all relevant factors
    All things considered, I think you were very
    lucky to have escaped injury when the plane
    crashed.

by all accounts
    from what one has heard
    By all accounts, it was the worst storm we've
    ever had in this area.

to tell you the truth
    to speak frankly
    Some friends have asked me to their party this
    evening, but to tell you the truth, I'd rather
    not go.

all the same
    nevertheless
    I know the other driver was going too fast, but
    all the same, by not stopping, you were partly
    to blame for the accident.

not to mention   also **let alone**
    even if we don't consider
    Increases in tax will be opposed by big business,
    not to mention small firms.

what's more
    furthermore
    I haven't got a television and what's more, I
    don't want one.

Complete the sentence

1. Spain is a good place to spend a holiday. For one thing...
2. Thatched roofs look nicer than tiled ones, but on the other hand...
3. I'd like two small loaves of bread. On second thoughts...
4. My job is very interesting. What's more...
5. The critics said that film was rubbish. All the same...

In your own words

1. (matter) I don't like the new manager. Neither, indeed, does anyone else.
2. (truth) I went to see the Picasso exhibition, but actually I didn't enjoy it.
3. (considered) Considering the cost, the itinerary and the service, I was very satisfied with my holiday.
4. (accounts) Everyone seemed to think it was an excellent play.
5. (mention) I'm looking forward to sunbathing, and of course swimming.

On your own

Make up sentences using these ten idioms.

SECTION 20.2

Find the idiom

1. After teasing the dog like that, he deserved to be bitten and I'm glad he was.
2. He isn't at all concerned whether he finds a job or not.
3. She thinks I deliberately misled her, but she's completely mistaken.
4. You don't have to go if you don't want to.
5. The fact that his brother is a Member of Parliament is irrelevant.

Ask and answer

1. (difference) Shall we have lunch in a pub or in a restaurant?
2. (business) How are you going to break the news to him?
3. (what) I had to sew a button on my jacket last night.
4. (helped) Were you sorry when you had to come home from holiday a week early? Yes, but ...
5. (things) Aren't you upset about your purse being stolen? No, not really, ...

On your own

Make up sentences using these ten idioms.

mind (one's) own business
not interfere or pry
He asked me how much I earned and I told him to mind his own business.

please (one)self
do as you like
'Would you like a cigarette?' 'No, thanks. Smoking is bad for the health.' 'Please yourself.'

(that's) neither here nor there
that's irrelevant, unimportant
'Can I borrow your car?' 'But you've never driven a Mini.' 'That's neither here nor there.'

couldn't care less
not care at all
I couldn't care less if I never see you again.

so what? also **what of it?**
what significance does that have? (implying no significance)
'Your mother disapproves of your behaviour.' 'So what? I'm not a child and I do as I please.'

nothing could be further from the truth
that's completely wrong
'But surely you were dismissed?' 'Nothing could be further from the truth. I left because I didn't like the way they operated.'

(it) serves (someone) right
someone deserves to suffer a bad result
'I was late for the play and they wouldn't let me in.' 'It serves you right. You're always late.'

(it) can't be helped
it can't be avoided or prevented
The concert has been cancelled because of the snow. It's a pity, but it can't be helped.

(it's) just one of those things
such things inevitably happen occasionally
We missed our plane because of the rail strike. It was just one of those things.

(it) makes no difference
it doesn't matter
It makes no difference whether the party is on Friday or Monday because I'm free both days.

SECTION 20.3

(it) stands to reason (that)
it's logical to conclude that
It stands to reason that people work harder if they enjoy their jobs.

(it) goes without saying (that)
it's obvious that
It goes without saying that if you retire early, you won't be entitled to a pension.

(it's) no wonder (that)
it isn't surprising that
It's no wonder that he has trouble with his liver. He drinks five pints of beer a day.

(it's) a good job (that)
it's fortunate that
It's a good job that the bus wasn't carrying any passengers when it crashed.

(it) just so happens (that)
in fact, although you may not realise this
'Look! We're running out of petrol. I told you we should have bought some at the last garage.'
'It just so happens that I have a spare can of petrol.'

(it's) just as well
it's fortunate in the circumstances
It's raining. It's just as well I remembered to bring my umbrella.

(it's) high time also **(it's) about time**
something must be done immediately (and should have already been done)
It's high time the council built a pedestrian crossing here. There have already been several accidents.

(it's) no secret (that)
it's a well-known fact that
It's no secret that this company has been losing money for several years.

rumour has it (that)
it's rumoured that
Rumour has it that a general election will be called this summer.

(I) take it (that)
I assume that
'What an awful noise!'
'I take it you don't like my new record.'

In your own words

1. (rumour) Lots of people seem to think the cricket tour will be cancelled.
2. (take) She assumed I was unhappy because I wasn't smiling.
3. (high time) We really must take those books back to the library immediately.
4. (wonder) I wasn't surprised when the river flooded after all that rain.
5. (job) It's lucky that I cooked plenty of food. I didn't know you were bringing friends home.

Complete the sentence

1. It ... that we'll celebrate your birthday, but what would you like to do?
2. It ... that you'll be tired after such a long walk.
3. It ... that you're getting married next month, you know.
4. It ... that I did pay the bill. I have the receipt in my pocket.
5. It ... that I decided not to work for that firm. They have just gone bankrupt.

On your own

Make up sentences using these ten idioms.

SECTION 20.4

Work it out

Try to work out the meanings of the idioms on this page from the example sentences and then write in the definitions. Check your answers in the key at the back of the book or in a dictionary.

On your own

Make up sentences using these ten idioms.

1. **can't stand**

   I can't stand having to be polite to people whom I dislike.

2. **can't help**

   I can't help smoking even though I know it's bad for my health.

3. **can't imagine**

   I can't imagine why you want to come into the office at weekends as well!

4. **wouldn't dream of**

   'Let me pay you for your help.'
   'I wouldn't dream of accepting payment from a friend.'

5. **(it's) no use** also **there's no use in**

   It's no use studying English if you never have a chance to use it.

6. **(it's) (well) worth**

   The cinema will be crowded, so it's worth making a seat reservation in advance.

7. **there's no harm in**

   I expect he'll refuse your request, but there's no harm in asking.

8. **there's no point in** also **see no point in**

   There's no point in going to the pub with us if you don't like drinking.

9. **(it) wouldn't do (for someone) to**

   It wouldn't do for the mayor to arrive late for the ceremony.

10. **(it) pays/doesn't pay to**

    It pays to have your car serviced regularly.

KEY

Unit 1, p. 9

1. explode
2. rise into the air
3. try to impress people
4. become cheerful, recover from depression
5. become calm
6. put on one's best clothes
7. expand the range of one's business
8. happen unexpectedly
9. faint
10. recover consciousness

Unit 2, p. 14

1. record spoken words in writing
2. delete
3. put clothes on to see if they fit
4. draft (a document, plan)
5. complete appropriate spaces (in a document, form)
6. distribute
7. withdraw (a statement, criticism)
8. mention (a subject)
9. make comfortable by using/wearing
10. purchase all available stocks

Unit 3, p. 19

1. do repeatedly
2. continue
3. continue
4. suddenly start
5. want to
6. choose, like
7. receive, inherit
8. want very much
9. reach the end of
10. consider something a bad thing

Unit 4, p. 24

1. leave
2. attend
3. become uncontrollable
4. try to notice
5. not go near
6. interrupt
7. do or get belatedly (news, sleep)
8. feel superior to
9. become involved or obsessed with
10. do (mischief)

Unit 5, p. 29

1. be forgotten
2. change one's idea or intention
3. decide
4. speak frankly
5. become insane
6. work as hard as one's fellows
7. withdraw one's remarks
8. be sufficient
9. achieve distinction
10. think hard

Unit 6, p. 34

1. assume control of
2. be offended by
3. look after
4. pity
5. acknowledge one's merit in doing
6. consider
7. be proud of
8. avenge oneself on
9. look enquiringly at
10. grasp

Unit 7, p. 39

1. lacking practice
2. not fit
3. breathless
4. unemployed
5. no longer fashionable
6. not generally available this season
7. uncharacteristic
8. no longer available (printed material)
9. no longer visible
0. not suited to (surroundings)

Unit 8, p. 44

1. old-fashioned
2. not working
3. not in control
4. not in contact
5. a forbidden area
6. no longer popular
7. not to be considered
8. no longer has a chance
9. mad, crazy
0. no longer in one's control

Unit 10, p. 54

1. satisfactory
2. absolutely (negative and interrogative only)
3. considered generally
4. as a summary or brief assessment
5. completely
6. within the limits of
7. on condition that
8. in order to
9. by a large margin
0. and other similar (things)

Unit 11, p. 59

1. an acceptable lie, told to avoid hurting someone's feelings
2. an area of countryside protected by law from building development
3. an illegal market
4. permission to do something
5. unnecessary bureaucracy
6. the times when commuters are travelling to and from work
7. a short route
8. a final burst of enjoyment
9. someone who has been doing the same job for a long time
10. unrealistic thoughts based on hopes rather than facts

Unit 13, p. 68

1. enable people at a social gathering to become relaxed
2. make peace
3. disturb a good arrangement
4. miss an opportunity
5. awaken a memory
6. become suspicious
7. become established
8. produce favourable results
9. make pedantic distinctions
10. exert influence through connections

Unit 14, p. 73

1. say or do exactly the right thing
2. reveal a secret
3. have a lifestyle where one does too many things at once
4. exaggerate the importance of something bad
5. escape from a bad situation into a worse one
6. have a bad secret
7. confront a difficulty instead of trying to escape from it
8. waste one's efforts on something that is already decided
9. reform one's character
10. misunderstand

Unit 16, p. 82

1. safely and without damage or injury
2. first and most important
3. fair and honest
4. out of bed and active
5. rare
6. in a final manner
7. generally speaking
8. damage from ordinary use
9. miscellaneous items of little value
10. every possible place of concealment

Unit 20, p. 99

1. hate
2. can't stop (oneself)
3. can't understand
4. wouldn't consider
5. it's useless to
6. it's advantageous to
7. there won't be any bad consequences even if it's ineffective
8. it's without purpose
9. it wouldn't be right to
10. it's/it isn't advantageous to

NDEX

NOTES